THE MAGIC FLUTE

THE MAGIC FLUTE

Wolfgang Amadeus Mozart

TEXT BY DAVID FOIL

Additional commentary by William Berger

BLACK DOG
& LEVENTHAL
PUBLISHERS
NEW YORK

Published by
Black Dog & Leventhal Publishers, Inc.
151 West 19th Street
New York, NY 10011

Distributed by
Workman Publishing Company
225 Varick Street
New York, NY 10014

Manufactured in China

Cover and interior design by Liz Driesbach

Cover image © Deutsches Theatermuseum, Munich, Germany/The Bridgeman Art Library

ISBN-13: 978-1-57912-759-6

h g f e d c b a

Library of Congress Cataloging-in-Publication Data available on file.

*I*magine that Wolfgang Amadeus Mozart decided to write a Broadway musical—a really great Broadway musical, of course—and you will understand what *The Magic Flute* is. It is a rollicking entertainment for the common man, only it is the work of an uncommon genius. The depth, the human drama, and the profound beauty Mozart discovers in this fairy-tale story come alive only when you can explore the action and the meaning behind the delightful melodies and heavenly sounds. The result is a musical theater piece that is silly, uproarious, fantastic, and frenetic while also being wise, perceptive, honest, and serene in its hope for mankind.

You will hear the entire opera on the two compact discs included on the inside front and back covers of this book. As you explore the book, you will discover the story behind the opera and its creation, the background of the composer, biographies of the principal singers and conductor, and the opera's text, or libretto, both in the original German and in an English translation. Special commentary has been included throughout the libretto to aid in your appreciation and highlight key moments in the action and the score.

Enjoy this book and enjoy the music.

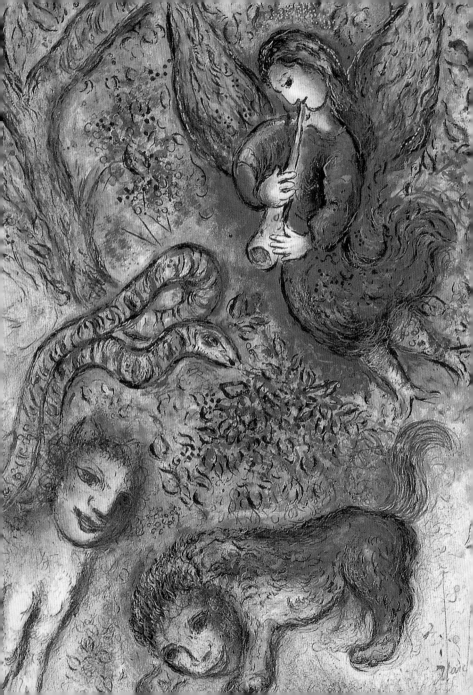

THE MAGIC FLUTE

*D*epending on your perspective, Wolfgang Amadeus Mozart's *Die Zauberflöte*—*The Magic Flute*—is either the silliest opera ever written or a work of profound insight that happens to be dressed in the trappings of a cartoon. Indeed, *The Magic Flute* is one of opera's fabulous anomalies. The opera was intended to be nothing more than a popular entertainment, but Mozart's genius elevated it beyond the realm of mere diversion. Its daft comedy and storybook romance hint at deeper, universal human concerns, while its swords-and-sorcerers plot

Left: Lithograph of *The Magic Flute* by Marc Chagall.
Above: Wolfgang Amadeus Mozart

is a striking metaphor for issues affecting the lives of Mozart and his librettist and leading man, Emanuel Schikaneder. The music is so blissfully melodic, so direct and crystalline in its expression, and yet so transcendent, that it confers grace, wit, and nobility on everything it touches. Yet, for all that, *The Magic Flute* was written to appeal to Everyman and Everywoman, and was performed in an atmosphere not unlike that of a Las Vegas dinner show.

Strictly speaking, it is not even an opera in the classical sense. In the Vienna of Mozart's day, opera was a fashion-conscious and carefully delineated medium cultivated to please the aristocracy, and the language of the text and performance was always Italian. Mozart wrote operas in the stately, elevated style called opera seria (*Idomeneo* and *La clemenza di Tito*); opera buffa, or comic opera (*Così fan tutte*); and something in between called dramma giocosa, or humorous opera with serious elements (*Don Giovanni*).

The Magic Flute—like its predecessor of a decade earlier, *The Abduction from the Seraglio*—was

The original playbill of *The Magic Flute*.

written to be performed in German, the common language of the people of Vienna. It also differs from most of Mozart's other stage works in that its musical numbers are linked with spoken dialogue instead of recitatives that are sung and accompanied by either orchestra or harpsichord. The Germans called this looser style *singspiel*, which translates loosely as "song play." The French term for it is opéra-comique; the English called it ballad opera; the Americans, musical comedy. Ironically, in spite of all of these distinctions, *The Magic Flute* was described hyperbolically in its original playbill as *Eine grosse Oper* (A Grand Opera). In his catalog, Mozart called it a "German opera," but the published libretto identified it, perhaps definitively, as a singspiel.

Mozart wrote his only other true singspiel, *The Abduction from the Seraglio*, in 1782 at the behest of the music-loving Hapsburg emperor Joseph II, who wanted a new stage piece written in German. The composer whipped up a giddy diversion that also took advantage of the contemporary rage in Vienna for anything Turkish—considered to be exotic—while showcasing the technical accomplishments of his singers. That last quality elicited a famous, perhaps apocryphal, exchange between sovereign and composer. "Too many notes, my dear Mozart," Joseph is reputed to have said, to which Mozart replied, "Exactly the right number, Your Majesty." Though *The Abduction from the Seraglio* proved to be a sizable hit, Mozart returned to the Italian style for the operas he wrote, amid dozens of other musical projects, in the 1780s. During that decade, he enjoyed tremendous success with the trio of operatic masterpieces he wrote with the brilliant librettist Lorenzo da Ponte—*Le nozze di Figaro*, *Don Giovanni*, and *Così fan tutte*, which were instantly acclaimed and frequently produced everywhere but in Vienna.

The charm of those heady days had faded by the time Mozart began working on *The Magic Flute*. He was thirty-five years old, and it was to be the last year of his life. Mozart (1756–1791), a celebrity performer and composer for hire for most of his life, emerged as a child prodigy at the keyboard when he was only four. He was renowned throughout Europe as a gifted boy, and matured almost seamlessly into the greatest composer of his age, even if the dimensions of his greatness were not fully recognized at the time. His life was difficult as an adult, especially when he became trapped in a miserable job as music master in the household of the prince-archbishop in his hometown of Salzburg. The prelate had little regard for music and seemingly less for Mozart himself. The composer's situation seemed to improve in 1781 when he finally escaped Salzburg for the cosmopolitan city of Vienna, the imperial capital of the Austrian Empire. There, his dazzling talent could not be ignored, and he enjoyed gratifying success as a composer in a variety of musical forms.

In many ways, however, Mozart was ill-equipped for the political intrigue and gossip that seems to be a venerable tradition in Viennese musical circles. He had an enemy in the more socially adept court composer Antonio Salieri, who enjoyed many of the privileges that eluded Mozart and may

Right: Mozart's birthplace, Salzburg.

well have conspired against him on occasion. Yet Mozart had an admirer in the emperor Joseph II, his patient if sometimes puzzled patron. Though Joseph II never went so far as to name Mozart court composer, he did commission Mozart and da Ponte to write *Così fan tutte* in 1789, and some believe he even suggested the plot to them.

Vienna's musical atmosphere changed abruptly in 1790 with the death of Joseph II; his successor, Leopold II, did not share his abiding love of music. Whatever chances Mozart might have had to curry favor with Leopold II—probably outside chances, at best—he seems to have bungled them in a series of political blunders that left him even further out of official favor than he had been before. Mozart lost his entrée at the Imperial Court, where he already had plenty of rivals, and could not generate much income from other sources. At the same time, he had to face the necessity of providing for his now-sizable family.

Enter Emanuel Schikaneder (1751–1812), an eighteenth-century Orson Welles, who could rightly be called an actor,

Right: Facade of the historic Theater an der Wien, Vienna.

Emal Schikaneder
als Fremder.

singer, composer, playwright, director, and entrepreneur. Though born into a poor family, the energetic Schikaneder was a self-made man and had known Mozart for years. The two met (and apparently played skittles on occasion) when the impresario's theatrical troupe was playing Salzburg in 1780, at the end of Mozart's miserable tenure there in the service of the city's prince-archbishop. Schikaneder's company had a sprawling repertoire that included everything from superficial stage spectacles to the tragedies of Shakespeare. Its performances made a strong impression on the composer, as did those of another company that had visited Salzburg the year before, suggesting to him the promise of a German-language national theater that would appeal to audiences of every class. Mozart and Schikaneder remained in occasional contact, and they also belonged to the same Masonic lodge in Vienna.

In the suburbs of Vienna, Schikaneder had erected a temporary performing space, the Theater an der Wien, that seated about one thousand people. The most popular of his shows there—singspiels—gave him ample opportunity to dazzle the audience with special effects, lavish scenery, sophisticated lighting, and live animal acts onstage. Interspersed among these spectacles were episodes of slapstick comedy, punctuated by songs the audience might leave the theater humming. The more unusual the show, the better, and Schikaneder found that tall tales told in extravagant and exotic settings added up to a good box office take. He called them "magic operas."

Just such a magic opera was what Schikaneder had in mind when he first discussed a new theatrical work with Mozart. It is possible that their discussions took place as much as a year before the premiere of *The Magic Flute*, but the actual writing and composition were accomplished fairly quickly in

One of the earliest piano scores of *The Magic Flute*, c. 1793.

A scene from a 1986 production of *The Magic Flute* at the Santa Fe Opera.

the summer and fall of 1791. How and why this collaboration developed into the remarkable work it is are questions still shrouded in mystery. There is little in the way of correspondence or other evidence to tell us why the creators made the choices they did. Schikaneder gets the sole credit for the libretto, but surely others, perhaps many others, had a hand in its completion.

And where did the story come from? There are a variety of sources that hint at the plot and the characters—an opera by an older contemporary of Mozart's named Johann Hiller; a then-popular book of fairy tales entitled *Dschinnistan* by Christoph Wieland; and any number of fables, folktales, and legends that both Schikaneder and Mozart were familiar with. But the sources are not as interesting as the guesswork that continues to this day about the stunning plot reversal that is introduced in the finale to Act I of *The Magic Flute*. Everything important in the plot up to that point is suddenly turned upside down: the much-feared Sarastro is revealed to be a heroic figure who presides over a noble and exclusive brotherhood, and the Queen of the Night—the erstwhile anguished mother of the kidnapped heroine Pamina—turns out to be a neurotic witch with a frightening agenda. Instead of vanquishing Sarastro at the Queen of the Night's request, the young prince Tamino, armed with the sound of the magic flute, agrees to be initiated into Sarastro's secret brotherhood.

The three boys in a production of *The Magic Flute* designed by Maurice Sendak for the Houston Grand Opera.

Why would Mozart and Schikaneder complicate their magic opera with such an incredible turn of events? We do not really know. We cannot underestimate the importance of the fact that both composer and librettist were Masons, a secret brotherhood in real life that was often under attack from the imperial household in Vienna and the Roman Catholic church. One of the Masonry's most powerful enemies was the Austrian empress Maria Theresa, who suppressed the order in 1764 and may have been the model for the Queen of the Night. The character of Tamino may be based on Maria Theresa's son, the beloved Joseph II, who reversed his mother's policy and was a friend and supporter of the Masons. The case can be made that almost every character in *The Magic Flute* has relevance to such dark political satire.

The whole work seems to turn on elements that come in threes. Three is a number of great significance in Masonic ritual and philosophy, so it is interesting to find the Three Ladies and the Three Boys in *The Magic Flute*, where Tamino—who learns the importance of the three qualities of virtue, discretion, and beneficence—must knock on three doors to enter three temples. In the score of the opera, the rituals of the brotherhood are punctuated by a threefold chord that is heard three times. Masons have historically felt a kinship with the message of the opera, and it is almost impossible to ignore the numerous Masonic references in the score and libretto.

Scene from the original production design of *The Magic Flute* after a 1795 etching by Josef and Peter Schaffer.

It is possible that Mozart simply wanted something a little more interesting than a conventional "magic opera," and insisted that he and Schikaneder play with the story elements. Whatever the reason, the ideals of an honorable fraternity as spoken and represented by Sarastro had a profound impact on Mozart, and this emerges in the beauty and nobility of his score. We can only imagine the misery he endured in 1791; he was unable to support his family properly and already weakened by an illness that would lead to the rheumatic fever which would kill him in December of that year. In spite of this demoralizing atmosphere, Mozart's productivity in 1791 was astonishing. In the months he worked on *The Magic Flute*, he also wrote—and these are only the highlights—his final opera seria, a splendid classical masterpiece entitled *La clemenza di Tito*; the

Clarinet Concerto; the exquisite motet "Ave verum corpus"; and the trunk of the unfinished *Requiem*.

Consider, too, that *La clemenza di Tito* and *The Magic Flute* had their debuts in the same month—September of 1791—in Prague and Vienna, respectively. Already ill and further debilitated by stress and travel, Mozart was at first rebuked in Prague, where he conducted the premiere of *La clemenza di Tito*. Attending were a pointedly unimpressed Leopold II and his empress; she described this sublime opera as "German swinishness" and said in a letter that it had put her to sleep. The general response was mixed at first, but Prague audiences had gradually come around to the beauties of *La clemenza di Tito* by its final performance. Mozart returned to Vienna in late September—in even worse health, but buoyed by the overall response he had received in Prague—determined to take care of the final details of *The Magic Flute*. It seems he wrote its overture in a single day, on September 28, two days before the premiere itself, which he conducted seated at the harpsichord.

The score for *The Magic Flute* is, from beginning to end, one of Mozart's most delightful creations. Aware of his audience and the nature of the theatrical material he was scoring, he consciously avoided writing anything that was complex or ambiguous. The music throughout is as lucid, as sharply defined, and as unmistakable as the signature chords that announce the overture, sketching and exploring the characters and situations in a deft but straightforward manner. The vocal demands vary, from the easily managed Papageno to the stratospheric heights of fancy reached by the Queen of the Night in her two

Leopold II, his wife, and some of their sixteen children.

arias. The first audiences at the Theater an der Wien must have been delighted with the abundance of quotable melodies, many of which became immediate hits with everyone in Vienna, from serious musicians to organ-grinders.

Onstage at the Theater an der Wien, *The Magic Flute* was a great success, one that Mozart reveled in, despite his weakened state. He attended a number of performances, often with a party of friends and admirers in tow, and took a proprietary interest in the audience's response. Of course, that audience was not as discriminating as the aristocratic crowd

Manuscript for Tamino's aria, "Dies Bildnis ist bezaubernd schön."

that had heard *La clemenza di Tito* or any of his Italian operas, and there is an interesting contemporary description of an infuriated Mozart chastising an audience member at the Theater an der Wien whom he thought had laughed in the wrong places during *The Magic Flute*. (He derisively called the man a "Papageno," after the jolly commoner who is the birdcatcher in *The Magic Flute*, the role Schikaneder himself played in the first performances.)

Right: Mozart was buried in 1791 in an unmarked grave in St. Mark's Cemetery in Vienna. Aficionados of his music erected this marker at his resting place in 1859.

Mozart knew that with *The Magic Flute* he had ventured into the realm of the silly and the fanciful—a tale of handsome princes and kidnapped virgins, shrewish queens and divine priests, magic flutes and bells, and trials by fire and water. But he found a miraculous connection, through all this stagecraft and whimsy, with the most profound aspects of the earthly quest for love, honor, truth, and wisdom. At the end of his life, Mozart's work had pushed past the limitations of an escapist trifle, and transcended the action of mere plot to plumb the depths and reach the heights of human longing and nobility.

THE STORY OF THE MAGIC FLUTE

Act 1

A handsome prince named Tamino runs across a wild and rugged plain, pursued by a hideous serpent. Overcome by the chase, he collapses. Just as the serpent is about to pounce on him, the Three Ladies who attend the Queen of the Night materialize and slay the serpent. Standing over the prostrate figure of the fallen hero, they argue over who will report his arrival to the Queen of the Night and who will stay to take care of him. They settle the matter by deciding that all three of them will make the report to the queen.

Tamino awakes alone, amazed to find the serpent dead at his feet. At that moment, Papageno wanders in. Lovesick and perpetually in search of the woman who will be his Papagena, he serves as a birdcatcher to the queen, who pays him in food and drink. Seeing an opportunity—and never being one to let an opportunity pass him by—Papageno grandly claims to

Construction of the serpent for Kautsky's 1912 set design for the Metropolitan Opera.

have slain the serpent himself. The Three Ladies return to catch him in his lie; they punish him by offering him water and a stone instead of wine and cakes, and slap a padlock on his mouth.

Turning to Tamino, they present him with a portrait of the beautiful Pamina, the daughter of the Queen of the Night. Arriving in ominous splendor, the Queen of the Night tells Tamino that Pamina is being held prisoner by the evil Sarastro. Before vanishing, the queen tells Tamino that if he saves her daughter, she will give him Pamina's hand in marriage.

From Act I of the Sendak-designed production at the Houston Grand Opera.

The Three Ladies remove the padlock from Papageno's mouth, telling him that he must now accompany Tamino on his mission to save Pamina. They give each of them a magic instrument—bells for Papageno and a flute for Tamino. The ladies tell them that the instruments will protect them from harm and that their guides will be the Three Boys.

Monostatos, Sarastro's Moorish servant, is making a bumbling attempt at seducing the horrified Pamina in his master's temple. Papageno stumbles in. Encountering each other for the first time, Monostatos and Papageno are terrified, and run in fear. Papageno, however, returns and tells Pamina why he has come. He explains Tamino's mission, and she joins him in marveling at the nature of human love.

Papageno bewitches Monostatos and his minions in the production of
The Magic Flute staged at the Lyric Opera of Chicago.

The Temples of Reason, Nature, and Wisdom as designed by
the artist David Hockney.

Tamino is led before the Temples of Reason, Nature, and
Wisdom by the Three Boys, who urge patience and steadfastness. Tamino's efforts to enter the temples are blocked until
the Speaker emerges from the Temple of Wisdom. The Speaker
tells Tamino that he has been deceived by the Queen of the
Night. Sarastro is no demon; he is instead the sovereign of the
Temple of Wisdom. The Speaker warns Tamino to put no trust
in a woman's word, meaning the Queen of the Night, and
returns to the temple, prevented by holy oath from saying

Left to right: Emmy Destinn as Pamina, Edward Lankow as Sarastro,
and Leo Slezak as Tamino in the Metropolitan Opera's original production of
The Magic Flute in 1912.

Left to right:
Mary Ellen Pracht,
Shirley Love, and
Gladys Kriese as
the three ladies in a
1950s production of
The Magic Flute.

more. Voices inform Tamino that Pamina is safe and that he will soon have the opportunity to gain wisdom. He plays his magic flute, hoping that Papageno and Pamina will hear him. Papageno answers with his panpipe, but he and Pamina miss the young prince in a trick of timing that has unfortunate consequences. Hearing the panpipe, Monostatos and his minions capture Papageno and Pamina. Papageno remembers his magic bells and plays them, bewitching Monostatos and his thugs, who dance happily.

Pamina sleeps in a Houston Grand Opera production of *The Magic Flute*.

Heralded by his followers, Sarastro sweeps into view, leaving a terrified Pamina to beg forgiveness for trying to escape. She explains Monostatos's assault on her just as the Moor arrives with Tamino, whom he has captured. Face to face for the first time, Tamino and Pamina rush into each other's arms, leaving Monostatos sputtering in rage. Sarastro rewards Monostatos with seventy-seven lashes. Sarastro blesses the young couple and bids them to submit to the trials of purification as his followers sing the praises of the lofty ideals that will transform earth into paradise.

Act 2

The Priests enter a sacred grove, in a solemn procession. Sarastro informs them that Tamino desires to join their brotherhood. He explains that it was preordained by the gods that Tamino would seek Pamina, and that this is the reason he took her from her formidable mother. The Two Priests are assigned to instruct Tamino and Papageno in the rituals before them, and all pause to offer prayers to the gods Isis and Osiris.

Night has descended on the courtyard of the temple when Tamino and Papageno, who is afraid of the dark, are brought in by the Two Priests and left by themselves. They are about to face the trials of initiation; the priests ask them once again if they are prepared to commit themselves. They answer that they are, though Papageno is not as convinced as Tamino, and they accept a vow of silence. Suddenly, the Three Ladies appear to lure them back into the spell of the Queen of the Night, but voices from the temple threaten the Ladies with everlasting damnation, and they flee.

In a garden, Pamina sleeps. Monostatos, who discovers her, salivates over her in this vulnerable state. But, his second chance to assault her is foiled by the arrival of the Queen of the Night.

Monostatos cowers in the shadows as, shrieking with fury, the queen raves about the way she has been betrayed and presents Pamina with a dagger with which the young woman is to assassinate Sarastro. When the queen vanishes once again, Monostatos steps forward, takes the dagger from Pamina, and tries to blackmail her into submitting to him. Sarastro enters suddenly. Pamina begs mercy for the queen. Sarastro calms her with his assurance that vengeance does not exist in his temple.

The Two Priests leave Tamino and Papageno in yet another solitary site within the temple. When Papageno whines for something to drink, an old woman appears with a cup of water. She is, she tells him, his lover, but a clap of thunder dismisses her before she can identify herself. The Three Boys return bearing the magic bells and the magic flute, and produce a sumptuous feast in an answer to Papageno's prayers. As the birdcatcher digs in, Tamino plays his flute, which summons Pamina. Tamino says nothing, adhering to his vow of silence, and Pamina departs in agony, believing that he no longer loves her. A threefold chord summons Tamino and Papageno to meet the challenges of the initiation.

Papageno (Otto Goritz) and Papagena (Bella Alten) in a 1912 production.

Scene from Act II in a Houston Grand Opera production designed by Maurice Sendak.

Within the sacred pyramid, the priests thank the gods for deeming Tamino worthy of their fraternity. He and Pamina are told to bid each other a final farewell, and they are separated. The priests leave, and Papageno stumbles in to find himself surrounded by fire. The Second Priest arrives to give him the bad news that he will not be among the initiates. Papageno does not care; all he wants is a glass of wine. He is given a drink, whereupon he relaxes enough to start longing once again for a wife. The old woman returns to tell Papageno that she must be his bride, or else he will be imprisoned forever. He accepts, and she is transformed into a beautiful girl, only to have the priests banish her immediately.

Pamina is heartsick, sure that her happiness is at an end. When she takes up the dagger the queen gave her, she means to kill herself, but the Three Boys, who have been monitoring her despair, intervene to reassure her that Tamino does indeed love her.

In the meantime, the young prince waits as the two Men in Armour prepare him for the trial of purification by fire and water. He hears Pamina's voice—she will join him in his quest. They endure the trials of fire and water without harm; Tamino plays his magic flute to spare them anguish and suffering.

Papageno is desolate, certain this time that he has lost his last chance for happiness. He is about to hang himself when the Three Boys hurry in to remind him that the magic bells will summon his beloved. The bells do the trick, and Papageno is at last happy with his Papagena.

The Queen of the Night, the Three Ladies, and Monostatos have banded together for one last attack on the temple, but thunder and lightning send them sprawling in ultimate defeat. From his temple, the wise and good Sarastro hails the victory of light over darkness, blessing the young lovers as his followers offer a hymn in praise of the wisdom and kindness of the gods.

THE PERFORMERS

ANNELIESE ROTHENBERGER (Pamina) was one of the most striking women on the operatic stage in the post–World War II era, enjoying an impressive career, based in her native Germany, that lasted over thirty years. Born in 1924 in Mannheim, Rothenberger began her studies there, making her operatic debut in 1943 in Koblenz, where she also appeared as an actress on the nonmusical stage. Three years later, she joined the ensemble of the Hamburg Opera, which essentially became her artistic home for the rest of her career. She added to her reputation throughout Germany with frequent radio appearances, and enjoyed her first international success with the Hamburg company on a 1953 visit to the Edinburgh Festival. Like many German singers of her day, Rothenberger's international reputation rested largely on Mozart and German roles by other composers; in Germany, she also sang much of the Italian and French lyric and coloratura soprano repertoire —but in German, which was the practice at the time. In 1954, she began making annual appearances at the Salzburg

Festival; she was also a frequent visitor to the Edinburgh and Aix-en-Provence festivals. Debuts at the Vienna Staatsoper, Milan's La Scala, and the Bavarian State Opera followed in the late 1950s. Most audiences today know Rothenberger for her performance as the youthfully radiant Sophie in the 1963 Salzburg Festival film of Richard Strauss's *Der Rosenkavalier,* starring Elisabeth Schwarzkopf. Rothenberger's charming appearance, infectious personality, and silvery voice often belied her intensely passionate approach to singing and acting; in fact, she would become highly respected for her portrayals of two very different women in Alban Berg's atonal operas—the tormented Marie in *Wozzeck* and the chillingly amoral title role in *Lulu.* She also created roles in new operas, such as Telemachus in Rolf Liebermann's *Penelope* and Agnes in Liebermann's *The School for Wives,* as well as the title role in Heinrich Sutermeister's setting of *Madame Bovary.* But it was in the operas of Mozart and Richard Strauss that she earned enduring acclaim outside Germany. Her 1960 Metropolitan Opera debut came in the role of Zdenka in Strauss's *Arabella* and, in Mozart's works, she was admired everywhere as Pamina, Susanna in *Le nozze di Figaro*, and Constanze in *The Abduction from the Seraglio*. Not unlike the prewar celebrities Maria Jeritza and Jarmila Novotna, beautiful sopranos who excelled in operetta as well as opera, Rothenberger recorded a great deal of operetta and appeared in a British film of Johann Strauss II's *Die Fledermaus*.

PETER SCHREIER (Tamino) began his career in 1944, at the age of nine, as one of the Three Boys in *The Magic Flute* at Dresden's Semper Opera House. Born near Meissen, he was at the time a boy contralto and member of the Dresden Holy Cross Church choir, with which he continued to sing even after his voice changed to tenor until 1954. Schreier pursued his musical studies after World War II in what was then known as East Germany. His intensive stage and musical training came from both the Dresden State Opera and Leipzig's renowned Hochschule für Musik. He sang in studio productions with the Dresden company and, in 1959, made his operatic debut there as an adult in the role of the First Prisoner in Beethoven's *Fidelio*. He became a full member of the Dresden company in 1961, winning acclaim with his performances of Mozart's works and other lyric tenor roles. In 1963, he also became a principal artist at the Berlin State Opera and began singing in other Eastern-bloc countries and the Soviet Union. Schreier's reputation also brought him to the West—especially after the sudden death of Fritz Wunderlich created a need for another

Peter Schreier as Tamino.

first-class lyric tenor in the German style. His first important Western engagement was with the Hamburg Opera, and he made his London debut in 1966 as Ferrando in *Così fan tutte*.

He began appearing regularly at the Salzburg Festival in 1967, which was also the year of his debuts with the Vienna Staatsoper and New York's Metropolitan Opera (where his debut role was Tamino). Subsequently, he appeared frequently with those companies and, after his debuts in 1969, with Milan's La Scala and Buenos Aires's Teatro Colón as well. Schreier's career has been a remarkably long and productive one, and his reputation as a lieder and oratorio singer has been as remarkable as his success in opera. As a recitalist, he has been recognized for his interpretations of the songs of Mozart, Franz Schubert, Robert Schumann, Johannes Brahms, and Strauss. His operatic repertoire was selective, relying heavily on German lyric-tenor roles and occasional forays into heavier repertoire (Max in *Der Freischütz* and the title role in Hans Pfitzner's *Palestrina*). Schreier was perhaps the definitive interpreter of his generation of the uniquely demanding roles of the Evangelist in Johann Sebastian Bach's *Passion of St. Matthew* and *Passion of St. John*. In the 1970s, he began conducting and made critically acclaimed recordings of choral works by Mozart and Bach, also appearing on some of them as a soloist.

KURT MOLL (Sarastro) has spent most of his illustrious career singing bass roles in the operas of Mozart, Richard Wagner, Strauss, and other Austrian and German composers. Rather than limiting him, this focus has allowed him to sing everything from raucously comic roles, such as Sir John Falstaff in Otto Nicolai's *The Merry Wives of Windsor* and Baron Ochs in Strauss's *Der Rosenkavalier*, to such noble paternal figures as

Kurt Moll as Sarastro.

the benevolent Sarastro in *The Magic Flute* and the patient, faithful Gurnemanz in Wagner's *Parsifal*. Combined with an artistry distinguished by its sensitivity and finesse, Moll's voice— sonorous, with the depth and tonal color of a true bass—is one of the most powerful and arresting of his generation. Born near Cologne in 1938, Moll became acquainted with music by playing the guitar and the cello and singing in the school choir. He studied at Cologne's Hochschule für Musik, making his professional debut at the Cologne Opera in 1958. After stints with a succession of provincial German opera companies—in Aachen, Mainz, and Wuppertal—Moll began a series of important debuts with the world's leading opera companies that established him as an important singer in his chosen repertoire. Since the late 1960s, he has been a regular visitor to the festivals at Salzburg and Bayreuth, as well as London's Covent Garden, Milan's La Scala, the Vienna Staatsoper, and the Paris Opéra. His American debut, in San Francisco in 1974, was in the role of Gurnemanz, and Wagnerian roles also introduced him to the Metropolitan Opera (Landgrave Hermann in *Tannhäuser*) and the Chicago Lyric Opera (Daland in *Der fliegende Holländer*). Moll is an admired concert and recital artist as well, and has recorded most of his signature roles.

WALTER BERRY (Papageno) was born in 1929 in Vienna, and his long career as a bass-baritone reflected the glory of the city's musical heritage. Berry was only in his early twenties when he made his first big impression at the Vienna Staatsoper as Figaro in Mozart's *Le nozze di Figaro*. As a teenager, after abandoning the idea of a career in engineering, he studied at the Vienna Academy of Music, which led to his entry into the company of the Staatsoper when he was only twenty-one. His success with the company brought him to the Salzburg Festival in 1952, and he became one of the mainstays of the festival's artist roster. In 1957, he married mezzo-soprano Christa Ludwig, and they became frequent collaborators onstage. He and Ludwig had a joint triumph as Barak the Dyer and the Dyer's Wife in Strauss's *Die Frau ohne Schatten*, which they sang in the Metropolitan Opera's historic 1966 production that served as Berry's house debut. In Germany and Austria, Berry and Ludwig frequently appeared together in German-language performances of operas (*Carmen*, for instance), but they did not perform elsewhere. Beginning in 1961, the Berlin Städtische Oper served as their artistic base, and their careers continued to run on parallel paths even after their divorce in 1970. An enormously charismatic singer, Berry was beloved in comic roles in Mozart operas, including Papageno and Figaro, Don Alfonso in *Così fan tutte*, and Leporello in *Don Giovanni*, and he also distinguished himself in the anguished title role of Berg's *Wozzeck*. While Berry's international career focused on lighthearted comic roles that did not always bring out the warmth and integrity of his voice, the sheer beauty and humanity of his singing emerged in his performances of the more serious and imposing concert and lieder literature of the great choral works of Bach, Joseph Haydn, Mozart, and Beethoven.

EDDA MOSER (Queen of the Night) had one of her greatest international successes in the brief but unforgettable role of the Queen of the Night, combining fierce grandeur and an almost Wagnerian intensity with an easy command of the hurtling, stratospheric coloratura in the character's two arias. The power and flexibility of her singing made Moser an unusually versatile operatic artist in a variety of coloratura and lyric-dramatic roles in both the mainstream repertoire and in new works. Born in Berlin in 1938, Moser is the daughter of the distinguished German musicologist Hans Joachim Moser. She began her professional career in 1962 in the small role of Kate Pinkerton in Giacomo Puccini's *Madama Butterfly* at the Berlin Städtische Oper. For most of the 1960s, Moser sang in provincial German houses before her promise was realized at the Frankfurt Opera during a three-year stint with the company (1968–71). She joined the Vienna Staatsoper shortly thereafter and became a regular at other German and Austrian houses as well as at the Salzburg Festival. Her 1968

Edda Moser as the Queen of the Night.

Metropolitan Opera debut came with the small role of Well-gunde in Wagner's *Das Rheingold*, but she was also acclaimed there in principal roles such as the Queen of the Night, Liu in Puccini's *Turandot*, and Donna Anna in Mozart's *Don Giovanni*.

WOLFGANG SAWALLISCH is perhaps the last of a line of great Austro-German conductors who came up through the ranks, beginning in the humble role of *répétiteur* (musical coach) in the network of provincial opera companies and ascending to international prominence in both the opera house and the concert hall. Much of Sawallisch's career has been centered in the city of Munich, where he was born in 1923. He began studying piano at the age of five and was immersed in private musical studies when he entered military service in 1942. At the war's end, Sawallisch finished his studies at Munich's Hochschule für Musik and, in 1947, took the position of répéti-teur at the Augsburg Opera, where he made his debut as a conductor in 1950. He moved through a series of increasingly important positions as musical director of opera companies in Aachen, Wiesbaden, and Cologne. Sawallisch made a sen-sational debut at the Bayreuth Festival in 1957 and became a regular visitor there for the next four seasons. He was appointed to his first major orchestral position in 1960 as principal con-ductor of the Vienna Symphony Orchestra, with which he made his American debut in 1964. As his international promi-nence grew, Sawallisch became one of the world's busiest conductors, holding jobs that frequently overlapped. In addi-tion to the Vienna post, which he held until the 1970s, he was musical director of the Hamburg State Philharmonic (1963–71), principal conductor of Geneva's Orchestre de la Suisse Romande (1970–80), and, beginning in 1971, musical director of Munich's Bavarian State Opera. In 1990, Sawallisch was named to succeed Riccardo Muti as musical director of the Philadelphia Orchestra, and officially assumed the post in 1993. In addition to his skill on the podium, Sawallisch is also a concert-worthy pianist who is one of the world's finest lieder accompanists in recitals and on recordings. He proved his versatility with a dazzling tour de force in Philadelphia during the winter of 1994: When a snowstorm depleted the ranks of the orchestra needed for a concert of Wagner operatic excerpts, Sawallisch had a piano rolled onstage and accompanied the singers himself.

The Libretto

Lucia Popp as the Queen of the Night in the 1967 Metropolitan Opera premiere of *The Magic Flute* designed by Marc Chagall.

Overture

Overture The three chords that sound the opening notes of the overture suggest an atmosphere of great sobriety and reverence. Trombones add to the depth of the sound, as does the adagio section (00:17) that follows immediately, with a few hints of the unexpected. The symbolism of "threes" is ever-present—the three opening chords, rising in thirds, are in the key of E-flat major, which contains three flats. An exhilarating chatter then breaks out (01:22) and spreads from the violins to the whole orchestra, sounding almost inappropriate and yet having an utterly delightful effect (01:56). Just as suddenly, the momentum is halted by the threefold chord in the winds (03:27) that will also signal a key moment in Act II. The orchestra seems to gossip in quiet response (03:50) in a series of minor-key episodes, before it returns to the major (05:06) and hurtles toward the finish (06:20) in the original key of E-flat major.

Act 1

DISC NO. 1/TRACK 2

Zu Hilfe! Zu Hilfe! **Listen to the beautifully articulate characterization of the Three Ladies who have saved Tamino's life (01:06). If you follow the libretto, you will see how completely and deftly Mozart succeeds in differentiating the three characters. The warm flow of melody and the interweaving of the voices of the Three Ladies as they fret about their next step (03:30) has a dazzling, sensuous effect that is typical of the whole score.**

SCENE ONE
Introduction

A clearing in a wild, rocky landscape.

Enter Tamino, coming down from a rock, with a bow but no arrows, and pursued by a serpent.

The Three Ladies stand behind the slain serpent in a 1795 etching by Josef and Peter Schaffer.

TAMINO	**TAMINO**
Zu Hilfe! Zu Hilfe! sonst bin ich verloren!	Help me! Oh, help me! or I am lost,
der listigen Schlange zum Opfer erkoren!	condemned as sacrifice to the cunning

Barmherzige Götter! Schon nahet sie sich! serpent!

Ach! rettet mich, ach! schützet mich! Merciful gods! It's coming closer!

Ah! save me, ah! defend me!

Three Ladies enter hurriedly, carrying silver javelins, as Tamino falls, unconscious, to the ground.

DIE DAMEN

Stirb, Ungeheu'r! durch unsre Macht!
Triumph! Triumph! Sie ist vollbracht,
die Heldentat! Er ist befreit
durch unsres Armes Tapferkeit!

THE LADIES

Die, monster! by our power!
Victory! Victory! Accomplished
is the heroic deed! He is set free
by the bravery of our persons!

ERSTE DAME

Ein holder Jüngling, sanft und schön —

FIRST LADY

A pleasing youth, gentle and fair—

ZWEITE DAME

So schön als ich noch nie gesehn!

SECOND LADY

Fairer than any I ever saw!

DRITTE DAME

Ja, ja gewiß, zum Malen schön!

THIRD LADY

Yes, that's true, fair enough to paint!

ALLE DREI

Würd' ich mein Herz der Liebe weihn,
so müßt' es dieser Jüngling sein.
Laßt uns zu unsrer Fürstin eilen,
ihr diese Nachricht zu erteilen.
Vielleicht, daß dieser schöne Mann
die vor'ge Ruh' ihr geben kann.

ALL THREE

If ever I gave my heart to love,
it could be to none but this youth.
Let us hurry to our Queen
and report this news to her.
It may be that this handsome man
may restore her former peace.

ERSTE DAME

So geht und sagt es ihr,
ich bleib' indessen hier!

FIRST LADY

Then go and tell her;
I'll stay meanwhile!

ZWEITE DAME

Nein, nein geht ihr nur hin.
ich wache hier für ihn!

SECOND LADY

No, no, you go ahead;
I'll keep watch here!

DRITTE DAME

Nein, nein, daß kann nicht sein,
ich schütze ihn allein!

ALLE DREI

Ich sollte fort? Ei, ei, wie fein!
Sie wären gern bei ihm allein.
Nein, nein, das kann nicht sein!
Was wollte ich darum nicht geben,
könnt' ich mit diesem Jüngling leben!
Hätt' ich ihn doch so ganz allein!
Doch keine geht; es kann nicht sein!
Am besten ist es nun, ich geh'.
Du Jüngling, schön und liebevoll
du trauter Jüngling, lebe wohl,
bis ich dich wiederseh'.

Exeunt all three.

THIRD LADY

No, no, that may not be;
I'll protect him by myself!

ALL THREE

Should I go then? Aha! how nice!
They would gladly be alone with him.
No, no, that may not be!
What would I not give
could I but live with this youth!
If only I could be alone with him!
Still they stay; it may not be!
It would be better if I go.
O youth, so fair and lovable,
O faithful youth, farewell!
until I see you again.

DISC NO. 1/TRACK 3

Wo bin ich? **The dazed Tamino hears the rustic panpipes (00:09) of Papageno, which will play throughout the opera.**

TAMINO *(erwacht)*

Wo bin ich?
Ist's Phantasie, daß ich noch
lebe? Wie? Die Schlange tot zu
meinen Füßen?

In the distance, the sound of panpipes.

Was hör ich?
Eine Gestalt nähert sich. Ich will sie von
ferne beobachten!

TAMINO *(coming to)*

Where am I?
Am I still alive, or is it my
imagination? What's this? The
serpent lying dead at my feet?

What is that I hear?
Someone is approaching. I'll hide and
observe him.

He hides behind a tree.

DISC NO. 1/TRACK 4

Der Vogelfänger bin ich ja Papageno is introduced with a robust tune of disarming simplicity, tweaked in each verse with the sound of the panpipes (00:18) with which he lures birds. Technically, the aria demands little of the baritone who sings it, but a great singer (such as Walter Berry in this recording) can invest it with an effervescent charm.

SCENE TWO
Song

During the introduction, Papageno comes down a footpath. On his back he is carrying a large birdcage containing various birds. He sings to the panpipes.

PAPAGENO	PAPAGENO
Der Vogelfänger bin ich ja,	Yes, I am the birdcatcher,
stets lustig, heißa hopsasa!	and ever merry—hopsasa!
Ich Vogelfänger bin bekannt	As birdcatcher am I known
bei alt und jung im ganzen Land.	by old and young throughout the land.
Weiß mit dem Locken umzugehn,	I know how to handle decoys
und mich aufs Pfeifen zu verstehn!	and whistle just like my prey!
Drum kann ich froh und lustig sein,	So I can be cheerful and gay,
denn alle Vögel sind ja mein.	for all the birds belong to me.
Der Vogelfänger bin ich ja,	Yes, I am the birdcatcher,
stets lustig, heißa hopsasa!	and ever merry—hopsasa!
Ich Vogelfänger bin bekannt	As birdcatcher am I known
bei alt und jung im ganzen Land.	by old and young throughout the land.
Ein Netz für Mädchen möchte ich,	I wish I had a trap for girls—
ich fing sie dutzendweis' für mich!	I'd catch them by the dozen, then!
Dann sperrte ich sie bei mir ein,	I'd keep them caged up at home,
und alle Mädchen wären mein.	and all the girls would be mine alone.
Wenn alle Mädchen wären mein,	If all the girls were mine alone,
so tauschte ich brav Zucker ein,	I'd trade some for the best sugar,

die, welche mir am liebsten wär,
der gäb' ich gleich den Zucker her.
Und küßte sie mit zärtlich dann,
wär' sie mein Weib und ich ihr Mann.
Sie schlief an meiner Seite ein,
ich wiegte wie ein Kind sie ein.

and then the one that I liked best—
I'd give her all the sugar she wanted.
And if she kissed me lovingly,
she'd be my wife and I her husband.
She would sleep at my side
and I would rock her like a child.

DISC NO. 1/TRACK 5

Meda! Was da?! Tamino meets his new companion Papageno, whose big mouth lands him in trouble—and not for the last time.

TAMINO
Heda!

TAMINO
Hey, you!

PAPAGENO
Was da?!

PAPAGENO
Who is there?

TAMINO
Sag mir, du lustiger Freund,
wer bist du?

TAMINO
Tell me, my merry friend,
who are you?

PAPAGENO
Wer ich bin? — Dumme Frage! —
Ein Mensch wie du. — Wenn ich dich nun
fragte, wer du bist.

PAPAGENO
Who am I?—*(Aside)* Stupid question!—
A human being like yourself. And what if
I asked you who you are?

TAMINO
Ich bin Prinz!

TAMINO
I am a prince!

PAPAGENO
Prinz?

PAPAGENO
A prince?

TAMINO
Sag, wovon lebst du?

TAMINO
Tell me, what do you live from?

PAPAGENO

Von Essen und Trinken, wie alle Menschen.

TAMINO

Und wodurch erhältst du das?

PAPAGENO

Ich fange für die sternflammende
Königin verschiedene Vögel, und dafür
erhalt' ich täglich Speise und Trank.

TAMINO

Sag mir, guter Freund,
warst du schon so glücklich,
diese Göttin der Nacht zu sehen?

PAPAGENO

Seh . . . ? Die sternflammende
Königin sehn? Sehn! Wa . . . warum blickst
du so verdächtig nach mir?

TAMINO

Weil ich zeifle, ob du ein Mensch
bist.

PAPAGENO

Was?

TAMINO

Nach deinen Federn, die dich
bedecken, da halt' ich dich . . .

PAPAGENO

Doch für keinen Vogel!
Du — du — du . . . bleib zurück, sag'

PAPAGENO

From food and drink, like everyone else.

TAMINO

And where do you get it from?

PAPAGENO

I catch birds for the starry Queen, and in
return she gives me my daily food and
drink.

TAMINO

Tell me, good friend,
have you ever had the good fortune
to see this goddess of the night?

PAPAGENO

See . . . ? See the starry Queen?
See her! but why are you looking at me
so suspiciously?

TAMINO

Because I'm dubious as to whether you are
a human being.

PAPAGENO

What?

TAMINO

Judging by the feathers you are covered in,
I think you are a . . .

PAPAGENO

Not a bird, I hope!
Just you keep your distance

ich, und traue mir nicht, denn ich —
ich habe Riesenkraft!

TAMINO

Riesenkraft? Also warst du wohl gar
mein Erretter, der diese giftiger Schlange
bekämpft hat?!

PAPAGENO

Schlange?—Ist sie tot oder lebendig?

TAMINO

Sie ist tot! Sag, wie hast du dieses
Ungeheuer bekampft?

PAPAGENO

Die — d . . . — erdrosselt!
(leise) Ich bin in meinem Leben noch nicht
so stark gewesen wie heut'.

Entrance of the Three Ladies.

DIE DAMEN

Papageno!

PAPAGENO

Ah! Das geht mich an!

TAMINO

Wer sind diese verschleierten Damen?

PAPAGENO

Na, das si . . . , also wer sie eigentlich
sind, weiß ich selbst nicht, ich weiß nur,
daß sie mir täglich meine Vögel abnehmen
und mir dafür süße Feigen bringen.

and don't trust me too far—I have the
strength of a giant!

TAMINO

The strength of a giant?
So you were the one who saved me from
this poisonous serpent, were you?

PAPAGENO

Serpent? Is it dead or alive?

TAMINO

It's dead! Tell me, how did you fight this
monster?

PAPAGENO

I—er—simply strangled it!
(Aside) I've never been so strong in all my
life as I am today!

THE LADIES

Papageno!

PAPAGENO

Excuse me, it's for me!

TAMINO

Who are these veiled ladies?

PAPAGENO

Well, they are . . . Well, I don't rightly
know who they are, actually; I only know
that they come every day and give me
sweet figs in return for my birds.

TAMINO

Sie sind vermutlich sehr schön?

PAPAGENO

Das glaub' ich nicht!
Eh, wenn sie so schön wären, würden sie
ihre Gesichter nicht bedecken.

DIE DAMEN

Papageno!

PAPAGENO

Oh je! — Hier, meine Schönen,
übergeb' ich meine Vögel.

ERSTE DAME

Dafür schickt dir unsere Fürstin
heute zum ersten Mal statt Wein reines,
helles Wasser!

She gives him a handsome bottle of water.

ZWEITE DAME

Und mir befahl sie, daß ich statt
Zuckerbrot diesen Stein dir überbringen
soll.

PAPAGENO

W — w — was? Steine soll ich fressen?

DRITTE DAME

Und statt der süßen Feigen,
habe ich die Ehre, dir dies goldene Schloß
vor den Mund zu schlagen.

TAMINO

I take it they are very beautiful?

PAPAGENO

I don't think so at all. After all, if they were
beautiful they wouldn't cover up their
faces.

THE LADIES

Papageno!

PAPAGENO

Oh dear! Here, my beauties, here are my
birds for you.

FIRST LADY

Today, for the first time, our Princess sends
you pure, clear water instead of wine.

SECOND LADY

And she commanded me to give you this
stone instead of the usual cake.

PAPAGENO

What's all this? I'm supposed to eat stones?

THIRD LADY

And instead of sweet figs, I have the
honour of stopping your mouth with this
golden padlock.

She snaps a padlock over his mouth.

PAPAGENO
Mmmmmmm . . .

ERSTE DAME
Damit du künftig nie mehr
Fremde belügst . . .

ZWEITE DAME
. . . und daß dich nie mehr der Heldentaten
rühmst, die andre vollbrachten.

PAPAGENO
Hm, hm, hm.

DRITTE DAME
Wir waren's, Jüngling, die dich
befreiten. — Hier dieses Gemälde schickt
dir die große Fürstin; es ist das Bildnis
ihrer Tochter Pamina. Findest du, sagte sie,
daß diese Züge dir nicht gleichgültig sind,
dann ist Glück, Ehr' und Ruhm dein Los.
Auf Wiedersehn! *(geht ab)*

ERSTE DAME
Auf Wiedersehn! *(geht ab)*

ZWEITE DAME
Adieu, Papageno! *(geht ab)*

PAPAGENO
Mmmmmmm . . .

PAPAGENO
Mmmmmmm . . .

FIRST LADY
So that in future you will never again tell
lies to strangers . . .

SECOND LADY
. . . and never again boast of heroic exploits
done by others.

PAPAGENO
Hm, hm, hm.

THIRD LADY
We were the ones, fair youth, who rescued
you. Here, our great Princess has sent you
this painting; it is a portrait of her
daughter Pamina. She said, if you are not
indifferent to these features, you will be
rewarded with happiness, fortune and
honour. Adieu! *(Exit.)*

FIRST LADY
Adieu! *(Exit.)*

SECOND LADY
Adieu, Papageno! *(Exit.)*

PAPAGENO
Mmmmmmm . . .

DISC NO. 1/TRACK 6

Dies Bildnis ist bezaubernd schön This is one of those moments that can make Mozart a terrifying experience for a singer. One of the most beautiful arias the composer ever wrote for the tenor voice, it requires that the singer have the utmost control of line (the way the notes are linked in a musical phrase) and plenty of breath, as well as a sense of rapturous awe (01:53). The voice is completely exposed (03:26), cradled in a simple, straightforward accompaniment. The aria is about beauty, and it must sound beautiful.

SCENE THREE
Aria

TAMINO

Dies Bildnis ist bezaubernd schön,
wie noch kein Auge je gesehn!
Ich fühl' es, wie dies Götterbild
mein Herz mit neuer Regung füllt.
Dies Etwas kann ich zwar nicht nennen,
doch fühl' ich's hier wie Feuer brennen.
Soll die Empfindung Liebe sein?
Ja, ja! Die Liebe ist's allein.
O wenn ich sie nur finden könnte!
O wenn sie doch hier vor mir stände!
Ich würde . . . würde warm und rein . . .
Was würde ich?
Ich würde sie voll Entzücken
an diesen heißen Busen drücken,
und ewig wäre die dann mein!

TAMINO

This portrait is bewitchingly fair,
such as no eyes have ever seen!
I feel this divine picture
filling my heart with a new emotion.
This Something I cannot name;
but I feel it here burning like fire.
Can this sensation be love?
Yes, yes! It can only be love.
Oh, if only I might find her!
If only she stood before me!
I would . . . would warmly, chastely . . .
What would I do?
I would, in my great delight,
press her to my ardent heart,
and make her mine forever!

Turns to go.

DISC NO. 1/TRACK 7

Rüste dich mit Mut und Standhaftigkeit. The Three Ladies return for Tamino and become shrill as thunder heralds the approach of their Queen.

Entrance of the Three Ladies.

ERSTE DAME
Rüste dich mit Mut und Standhaftigkeit,
schöner Jüngling!

FIRST LADY
Arm yourself with courage and
steadfastness, fair youth!

ZWEITE DAME
Die Fürstin hat jedes deiner
Worte gehört . . .

SECOND LADY
The Princess has heard your every
word.

DRITTE DAME
Hat dieser Jüngling, sprach sie, auch soviel
Mut und Tapferkeit, als er zärtlich ist, so ist
meine Tochter gewiß gerettet.

THIRD LADY
She said, if this youth is as bold and brave
as he is handsome, my daughter will defi-
nitely be rescued.

TAMINO
Wo ist sie?

TAMINO
Where is she?

ERSTE DAME
Ein mächtiger Herrscher hat sie
ihrer Mutter entrissen.

FIRST LADY
A powerful ruler has abducted her from her
mother.

TAMINO
Kommt, Mädchen, führt mich!
Pamina sei gerettet! *(Donner)*
Was ist das?

TAMINO
Come, ladies, lead me to her!
Let Pamina be rescued. *(Thunder.)*
What is that?

ERSTE DAME
Es verkündet die Ankunft
unserer Königin! *(Donner)*

FIRST LADY
It heralds the arrival of our Queen.
(Thunder.)

DIE DRIE DAMEN
Sie kommt! — Sie kommt!
— Sie kommt! *(Donner; es wird Nacht.)*

THE THREE LADIES
She comes, she comes, she comes!
(Thunder. Night falls.)

O zittre nicht, mein lieber Sohn! The Queen of the Night appears in an august, if ominous, manner, and grandly begins her aria (00:23), pouring out her anguish to Tamino. When she begins to insist that he save Pamina (03:24), a rattling, neurotic bitterness possesses her, taking the form of malevolent but spellbinding stratospheric coloratura writing (03:53). Though its high notes and intricate writing attract lighter voices, the role of the Queen of the Night is best filled by a dramatic soprano, such as Edda Moser on this recording, who has solid high notes, flexibility, and a forceful voice.

SCENE FOUR
Recitative and Aria

KÖNIGIN	**QUEEN**
O zittre nicht, mein lieber Sohn!	O tremble not, beloved son!
du bist unschuldig, weise, fromm.	You are guiltless, wise and good.
Ein Jüngling, so wie du, vermag am besten,	A youth such as you can best console
dies tiefbetrübte Mutterherz zu trösten.	this sorely distressed mother's heart.
Zum Leiden bin ich auserkoren;	I am condemned to grief,
denn meine Tochter fehlet mir.	for my daughter is taken from me.
Durch sie ging all mein Glück verloren,	In her is all my happiness lost,
ein Bösewicht entfloh mit ihr.	a villain has stolen her away.
Noch seh' ich ihr Zittern	I still can see her trembling
mit bangem Erschüttern,	with deep agitation,
ihr ängstliches Beben,	her fearful shaking,
ihr schüchternes Streben!	her modest struggles!
Ich mußte sie mir rauben sehen.	I had to endure seeing her taken.
»Ach helft!« war alles, was sie sprach;	"Ah, help!" was all that she could say;
allein vergebens war ihr Flehen,	but in vain were all her tears,
denn meine Hilfe war zu schwach.	for my aid was far too weak.
Du wirst sie zu befreien gehen,	You shall go to set her free,
du wirst der Tochter Retter sein!	you shall be my daughter's saviour!
Und werd' ich dich als Sieger sehen,	And when I see you victorious,
so sei sie dann auf ewig dein!	then shall she be yours forever!

Exeunt Queen and Ladies. Daylight returns.

DISC NO. 1/TRACKS 9 – 11

Ist denn auch Wirklichkeit, was ich sah? **The plot moves forward significantly in this delightful ensemble, in which Tamino and the hapless Papageno learn what is expected of them
(00:41). The whole quintet is a superb example of Mozart's theatrical genius—the music is
radiantly light and witty (04:29), yet without a wasted breath or gesture, qualities that can
also be heard in the following trio with Papageno, Monostatos, and Pamina (Track 11).**

TAMINO	**TAMINO**
Ist denn auch Wirklichkeit, was ich sah?	Was what I saw real?
Ihr guten Götter, täuscht mich nicht!	O you good gods, do not deceive me!

Papageno steps forward again.

SCENE FIVE
Quintet

PAPAGENO	**PAPAGENO**
Hm! hm! hm! hm!	Hm! hm! hm! hm!

TAMINO	**TAMINO**
Der Arme kann von Strafe sagen,	The poor fellow may well tell of punishment,
denn seine Sprache ist dahin!	for they have made him speechless!
Ich Kann nichts tun, als dich beklagen,	I can do nothing but pity you,
Weil ich zu schwach zu helfin bin.	for I am too weak to help.

The Three Ladies return, and the first removes his padlock.

ERSTE DAME	**FIRST LADY**
Die Königin begnadigt dich,	The Queen has mercy on you,
erläßt die Strafe dir durch mich.	and lifts her punishment through me.

PAPAGENO

Nun plaudert Papageno wieder.

ZWEITE DAME

Ja, plaudre, lüge nur nicht wieder.

PAPAGENO

Ich lüge nimmermehr, nein, nein!

DIE DAMEN

Dies Schloß soll deine Warnung sein.

PAPAGENO

Dies Schloß soll meine Warnung sein.

ALLE

Bekämen doch die Lügner alle
ein solches Schloß vor ihren Mund!
Statt Haß, Verleumdung, schwarzer Galle,
bestünde Lieb' und Bruderbund.

ERSTE DAME

O Prinz, nimm dies Geschenk von mir,
dies sendet unsre Fürstin dir.
Die Zauberflöte wird dich schützen,
im größten Unglück unterstützen.

DIE DAMEN

Hiermit kannst du allmächtig handeln,
der Menschen Leidenschaft verwandeln,
der Traurige wird freudig sein,
den Hagestolz nimmt Liebe ein.

ALLE

O! so eine Flöte ist mehr

PAPAGENO

Now Papageno can chatter again.

SECOND LADY

Yes, chatter, but never lie again.

PAPAGENO

Nevermore will I lie, no, never!

THE LADIES

This lock shall be your warning.

PAPAGENO

This lock shall be my warning.

ALL

If only every liar received
such a padlock over his mouth!
Then hate, calumny, black rancour
would change to love and brotherhood.

FIRST LADY

O Prince, take this gift from me,
sent to you by our lady.
This magic flute will protect you
though cast down in greatest misfortune.

THE LADIES

With it you can deal mightily,
transform the sorrows of mankind;
the mourner will become merry,
the old bachelor will turn to love.

ALL

Oh! such a flute is more

als Gold und Kronen wert,
denn durch sie wird Menschenglück
und Zufriedenheit vermehrt.

PAPAGENO
Nun, ihr schönen Frauenzimmer,
darf ich? So empfehl' ich mich.

DIE DAMEN
Dich empfehlen kannst du immer,
doch bestimmt die Fürstin dich,
mit dem Prinzen ohn' Verweilen,
nach Sarastros Burg zu eilen.

PAPAGENO
Nein! dafür bedank' ich mich!
Von euch selbsten hörte ich,
daß er wie ein Tigertier;
sicher ließ ohn' alle Gnaden
mich Sarastro rupfen, braten,
setzte mich den Hunden für!

DIE DAMEN
Dich schützt der Prinz, trau ihm allein!
dafür sollst du sein Diener sein.

PAPAGENO
(Daß doch der Prinz, beim Teufel wäre!
Mein Leben ist mir lieb;
am Ende schleicht, bei meiner Ehre,
er von mir wie ein Dieb.)

The first Lady gives Papageno a small chest of bells.

ERSTE DAME
Hier, nimm dies Kleinod, es ist dein.

---

precious than gold or crowns,
for by its power will human joy and
contentment be increased.

PAPAGENO
Now, fair ladies,
may I? Thus I take my leave.

THE LADIES
Another time you may depart,
but now our lady elects you
to accompany the prince
in haste to Sarastro's citadel.

PAPAGENO
No! I thank you very much!
I heard it from you yourselves,
that he is like a wild tiger;
surely in cold blood Sarastro
would have me plucked and roasted,
and thrown down for dogs to eat!

THE LADIES
The Prince will protect you, trust in him!
So that you may be his man.

PAPAGENO
(The devil take this Prince away!
My life is precious to me,
and now, by my honour, it's stealing
away from me like a thief.)

FIRST LADY
Here, take this treasure, it is yours.

PAPAGENO
Ei! ei! was mag darinnen sein?

PAPAGENO
Aha! what can it be?

DIE DAMEN
Darinnen hörst du Glöckchen tönen.

THE LADIES
Inside you can hear bells ringing.

PAPAGENO
Werd' ich sie auch wohl spielen können?

PAPAGENO
And shall I be able to play them?

DIE DAMEN
O ganz gewiß, ja! ja! gewiß.

THE LADIES
Oh, for certain, yes, for certain!

ALLE
Silberglöckchen, Zauberflöten
sind zu eurem (unserm) Schutz vonnöten,
Lebet wohl! wir wollen gehn
lebet wohl! auf Wiedersehn.

ALL
Silver bells, the magic flute
will be needful for protection.
Farewell! we go now;
farewell! till we meet again.

The Three Ladies turn to go.

TAMINO
Doch, schöne Damen, saget an —

TAMINO
But fair ladies, tell me—

TAMINO UND PAPAGENO
Wie man die Burg wohl finden kann?

TAMINO AND PAPAGENO
How will we find that citadel?

DIE DAMEN
Drei Knaben, jung, schön, hold und weise,
umschweben euch auf eurer Reise,
sie werden eure Führer sein;
folgt ihrem Rate ganz allein.

THE LADIES
Three boys, young, fair, gentle and wise,
will appear to you on your journey.
They will be your guides;
follow their counsels and none other.

TAMINO UND PAPAGENO
Drei Knaben, jung, schön, hold und weise,
umschweben uns auf unsrer Reise.

TAMINO AND PAPAGENO
Three boys, young, fair, gentle and wise,
will appear to us on our journey.

DIE DAMEN	**THE LADIES**
Sie werden eure Führer sein;	They will be your guides;
folgt ihrem Rate ganz allein.	follow their counsels and none other.
ALLE	**ALL**
So lebet wohl! wir wollen gehn,	So farewell! we go now;
lebt wohl! auf Wiedersehen.	farewell! until we meet again.

Exeunt.

The scene changes to a splendid chamber in Sarastro's palace.

Enter Monostatos. Pamina is led by slaves.

SCENE SIX
Trio

MONOSTATOS	**MONOSTATOS**
Du feines Täubchen, nur herein!	My fine little dove, come inside!
PAMINA	**PAMINA**
O welche Marter! welche Pein!	Oh, what suffering! what pain!
MONOSTATOS	**MONOSTATOS**
Verloren ist dein Leben!	Your life is lost!
PAMINA	**PAMINA**
Der Tod macht mich nicht beben,	Death does not make me tremble—
nur meine Mutter dauert mich,	I sorrow only for my mother;
sie stirbt vor Gram ganz sicherlich.	she will surely die of grief.
MONOSTATOS	**MONOSTATOS**
He! Sklaven! legt ihr Fesseln an!	Hey, slaves! Put her in chains!
Mein Haß soll dich verderben!	My hate will be your ruin!

PAMINA

O laß mich lieber sterben,
weil nichts, Barbar! dich rühren kann.

PAMINA

O let me rather die,
barbarian! for no emotion touches you!

MONOSTATOS

Nun fort! nun fort! Laßt mich mit ihr
allein.

MONOSTATOS

And now get out! Leave me alone
with her.

She falls unconscious on the sofa, as the Slaves hurry out of the room. Papageno appears outside at the window, as yet unnoticed by Monostatos.

PAPAGENO

Wo bin ich wohl? Wo mag ich sein?
Aha! da find' ich Leute. Gewagt! ich geh'
hinein. *(Tritt ein)*
Schön Mädchen, jung und fein, viel weißer
noch als Kreide —

PAPAGENO

Where am I? Wherever may I be?
Aha! there's someone there. Risky, but I'll
go in. *(He enters.)*
Pretty maiden, young and fair,
whiter even than chalk—

Papageno and Monostatos come face to face and both are terrified.

PAPAGENO UND MONOSTATOS

Hu! das ist der Teufel sicherlich!
Hab Mitleid! verschone mich! Hu! Hu!

PAPAGENO AND MONOSTATOS

Oo! That is surely none but the Devil!
Have pity! spare me! Oo! Oo!

They both run off.

DISC NO. 1/TRACK 12

Mutter! Mutter! Pamina and Papageno discover they have much in common. Despite their
different backgrounds, both are searching for love.

PAMINA *(erwacht)*

Mutter! Mutter! —
Wie, noch schlägt dieses Herz! —
Zu neuen Qualen erwacht. Oh, das is hart,
mir bitterer als der Tod.

PAMINA *(coming to)*

Mother, Mother!
What's this? My heart is still beating!
Awoken to new torments? Oh, that is
cruel; bitterer than death itself.

PAPAGENO *kommt zurück*
Bin ich nicht ein
Narr, daß ich mich schrecken ließ? —
Es gibt doch schwarze Vögel in der Welt,
warum nicht auch schwarze Menschcen.
— Ah, da ist das schöne Fräuleinbild noch.
— Du, Tochter der nächtlichen Königin . . .

PAMINA
Nächtliche Königin? —
Wer bist du?

PAPAGENO
Ein Abgesandter der sternflammenden
Königin.

PAMINA
Meiner Mutter?

PAPAGENO
Ja.

PAMINA
Dein Name?

PAPAGENO
Papageno.

PAMINA
Papageno?! Oh, ich erinnere mich
dein Namen oft gehört zu haben, dich
selbst aber sah ich noch nie.

PAPAGENO
Ich dich ebensowenig.

PAPAGENO *returns*
I'm a fool to be so
frightened, aren't I? After all, there are
blackbirds in this world, why not black
people, too?
Oh, look, that lovely girl is still there.
I say, daughter of the Queen of the Night!

PAMINA
Queen of the Night?
Who are you?

PAPAGENO
An envoy from the starry Queen.

PAMINA
My mother?

PAPAGENO
Yes.

PAMINA
What is your name?

PAPAGENO
Papageno.

PAMINA
Papageno? I remember hearing the name
quite often, but I have never seen you
before.

PAPAGENO
I have never seen you before either.

PAMINA

Du kennst also meine gute, zärtliche
Mutter?

PAPAGENO

Wenn du die Tochter der
nächtlichen Königin bist — ja.

PAMINA

Oh, ich bin es.

PAPAGENO

Das werde ich gleich nach diesem bild
erkennen die Augen braun, — richtig,
braun, — Lippen rot, — richtig, rot, —
blonde Haare — blonde Haare, alles trifft
ein, bis auf Hände und Füße, nach diesem
Gemälde solltest du weder Hände noch
Füße haben.

PAMINA

Erlaube mir?! Ja, ich bin's!

PAPAGENO

Ha!

PAMINA

Doch wie kam es in dein Hände?

PAPAGENO

Ich kam heute früh wie gewöhnlich
zu deiner Mutter Palast, eben als ich im
Begriffe war, meine Vögel abzugeben, da
sah ich einen Menschen vor mir, der sich
Prinz nennen läßt.

PAMINA

So you know my good and gentle mother?

PAPAGENO

If you are the daughter of the Queen of the
Night, yes.

PAMINA

Oh, I am!

PAPAGENO

I shall soon see by comparing you with
this picture. Eyes brown — yes, brown.
Lips red — yes, red. Blond hair — yes,
blond hair.
Everything fits, except the hands and feet.
According to this painting,
you shouldn't have any hands or feet.

PAMINA

May I see? Yes, it's me!

PAPAGENO

See!

PAMINA

But how did you get hold of it?

PAPAGENO

I went to your mother's palace this morning
as usual, and just as I was about to
deliver my birds, I saw a young man
before me who called himself
a prince.

PAMINA

Ein Prinz?

PAPAGENO

Ja! Dieser Prinz hat deine Mutter so für
sich eingenommen, daß sie ihm dein
Bildnis schenkte und ihm befahl, dich zu
befreien.

PAMINA

Mich zu befreien?!

PAPAGENO

Pscht! Sein Entschluß war so
schnell wie seine Liebe zu dir.

PAMINA

Er liebt mich also?

PAPAGENO

Mm. Komm, du wirst Augen machen,
wenn du den schönen Jüngling erblickst.

PAMINA

Wohlan denn, es sei gewagt!
Aber wenn dies ein Fallstrick wäre? Wenn
dieser
ein böser Geist aus Sarastros Gefolge wäre?

PAPAGENO

Ich? ein böser Geist?

PAMINA

Hm!

PAMINA

A prince?

PAPAGENO

Yes, and this prince so captivated your
mother that she gave him your
portrait and commanded him to rescue
you.

PAMINA

To rescue me?

PAPAGENO

Why, his determination to do so was as
sudden as his falling in love with you.

PAMINA

He loves me?

PAPAGENO

Mm. Come, you will be all eyes when you
see the fair youth.

PAMINA

Let's go, then, and risk it!
But suppose this should be a trap?
What if this man were an evil genius,
one of Sarastro's minions?

PAPAGENO

Me, an evil genius?

PAMINA

Mm.

PAPAGENO

Wo denkst du hin? Bei mir ist von
Geist keine Spur!

PAMINA

Vergib, Freund, wenn ich dich
beleidigte? Du hast ein gefühlvolles Herz.

PAPAGENO

Freilich hab' ich ein gefühlvolles
Herz, was nützt mir das alles. Ich möchte
mir oft alle meine Federn ausrupfen, wenn
ich bedenke, daß Papageno noch keine
Papagena hat.

PAMINA

Armer Mann, du hast also noch kein Weib?

PAPAGENO

Noch nicht einmal ein Mädchen,
viel weniger ein Weib, und unsereiner hat
auch bisweilen so seine lustigen Stunden,
wo man gerne . . . gesellschaftliche
Unterhaltung pflegen möchte.

PAMINA

Geduld, Freund, der Himmel wird auch
für dich sorgen. Er wird dir eine Freundin
schicken, ehe du dir's vermutest.

PAPAGENO

Wenn er sie nur bald schickte!

PAPAGENO

What are you thinking of?
I haven't a trace of genius in me!

PAMINA

Forgive me, my friend, if I offended you.
You have a tender heart.

PAPAGENO

Indeed I have a tender heart.
But what good does it do me? I often feel
like plucking out all my feathers when I
consider that Papageno still hasn't a
Papagena.

PAMINA

Poor man, haven't you found a wife yet?

PAPAGENO

Not even a girlfriend, let alone a wife.
And after all, yours truly also has the
urge sometimes to have a bit of
company and enjoy
himself.

PAMINA

Patience, my friend, heaven will provide
for you, too. It will send you a girlfriend
sooner than you expect.

PAPAGENO

If only it would send her now!

Bei Männern, welche Liebe fühlen The direct, unpretentious nature of singspiel might have inspired Mozart to cast this beguiling duet in the form of a hymn. It is a moment of great tenderness and humanity: Together the princess Pamina and the birdcatcher Papageno wonder at the spiritual nature of the love between a man and a woman, with her voice virtually taking flight (02:35) and his more earthbound expression echoing hers.

SCENE SEVEN
Duet

PAMINA
Bei Männern, welche Liebe fühlen,
fehlt auch ein gutes Herze nicht.

PAPAGENO
Die süßen Triebe mitzufühlen,
ist dann der Weiber erste Pflicht.

BEIDE
Wir wollen uns der Liebe freun,
wir leben durch die Lieb' allein.

PAMINA
Die Lieb' versüßet jede Plage,
ihr opfert jeder Kreatur.

PAPAGENO
Sie würzet unsre Lebenstage
sie wirkt im Kreise der Natur.

BEIDE
Ihr hoher Zweck zeigt deutlich an,
nichts Edlers sei als Weib und Mann.
Mann und Weib, und Weib und Mann

PAMINA
In men who know the feeling of love
good hearts cannot be lacking.

PAPAGENO
Returning their sweet desires
is then the first duty of womankind.

BOTH
We gladly rejoice in Love's power,
and live by love alone.

PAMINA
Love can sweeten every trouble;
all creatures sacrifice to it.

PAPAGENO
It seasons every day of our lives,
and turns the wheels of all Nature.

BOTH
Its higher purpose makes it clear
that nothing is nobler than man and
woman. Man and woman, and woman and

| reichen an die Gottheit an. | man, attain the level of divinity. |
| *Beide ab.* | *Exeunt.* |

The scene changes to a grove. In the centre background is a beautiful temple, with the inscription "Temple of Wisdom." This temple is joined by colonnades to two others; one of them has the inscription "Temple of Reason," the other, "Temple of Nature."

Three Boys lead in Tamino; each holds a silver palm-leaf in his hand.

DISC NO. 1/TRACKS 14 & 15

Act I Finale The ethereal sounds of the Three Boys begin this extended finale. Tamino uses his magic flute to charm the wild animals (track 15). Tamino begins to learn that things are not quite as the Queen of the Night and her Three Ladies had led him to believe. We finally meet the much-maligned Sarastro: With a flourish of trumpets and drums (06:50), he appears in a chariot drawn by lions. He turns out to be a great and good man, determined to break the power of the malignant Queen of the Night. Mozart characterizes him with great affection and dignity—listen to the serene, rock-solid certainty of his song, delivered in a sonorous bass voice (08:31), as the first act sweeps to a magnificent conclusion.

SCENE EIGHT
Finale

DIE DREI KNABEN	**THE THREE BOYS**
Zum Ziele führt dich diese Bahn,	This path will lead you to your goal,
doch mußt du, Jüngling, mannlich siegen.	yet, youth, you must strive like a man.
Drum höre unsre Lehre an:	So give heed to our teaching
Sie standhaft, duldsam und verschwiegen!	Be steadfast, patient and keep silence!

TAMINO	**TAMINO**
Ihr holden Kleinen, sagt mir an,	You gracious lads, tell me first
ob ich Paminen retten kann?	shall I be able to save Pamina?

A resplendent Sarastro in a 1984 production at the Santa Fe Opera.

KNABEN

Dies kundzutun steht uns nicht an
Sei standhaft, duldsam und verschwiegen!
Bedenke dies; kurz, sei ein Mann!
Dann, Jüngling, wirst du männlich siegen.
(Beide ab.)

TAMINO

Die Weisheitslehre dieser Knaben
sei ewig mir ins Herz gegraben!
Wo bin ich nun? Was wird mit mir?
Ist dies der Sitz der Götter hier?
Doch zeigen die Pforten, es zeigen die
Säulen, daß Klugheit und Arbeit und
Künste hier weilen; wo Tätigkeit thronet
und Müßiggang weicht,

BOYS

We are not free to make that known
Be steadfast, patient and keep silence!
Remember this; in short, be a man!
Then, youth, you will strive manfully.
(Exeunt.)

TAMINO

May the wise teachings of these boys be
ever engraved in my heart!
Where am I now? What will happen to me?
Is this the domain of the gods?
These portals, these columns prove
that skill, industry, art reside here;
where action rules and idleness is banished
vice cannot easily gain control.

erhält seine Herrschaft das Laster nicht leicht. Ich wage mich mutig zur Pforte hinein; die Absicht ist edel und lauter und rein. Erzittre, feiger Bösewicht! Paminen retten ist mir Pflicht!

I will boldly pass through that portal; my purpose is noble, straightforward, pure. Tremble, cowardly villain! My duty is to save Pamina!

He approaches the portal at one side. A voice from inside warns him back.

EINE STIMME
Zurück!

A VOICE
Go back!

TAMINO
Zurück? So wag' ich hier mein Glück.

TAMINO
Go back? Then I will try my luck here.

He approaches the portal at the opposite side.

EINE STIMME
Zurück!

A VOICE
Go back!

TAMINO
Auch hier ruft man »zurück«?
Da seh' ich noch eine Tür!
Veilleicht find' ich den Eingang hier.

TAMINO
Here too they call "go back"?
Still I see one more door!
Perhaps here I will find entrance.

As he knocks at the portal in the center, an old Priest appears.

SPRECHER
Wo willst du, kühner Fremdling hin?
Was suchst du hier im Heiligtum?

SPEAKER (*Priest*)
Where would you enter, bold stranger?
What do you seek in this holy place?

TAMINO
Der Lieb und Tugend Eingentum.

TAMINO
What belongs to Love and Virtue.

SPRECHER
Die Worte sind von hohem Sinn,

SPEAKER
Your words are lofty ones,

allein, wie willst du diese findenn?
Dich leitet Lieb' und Tugend nicht,
weil Tod und Rache dich entzünden.

TAMINO
Nur Rache für den Bösewicht!

SPRECHER
Den wirst du wohl bei uns nicht finden.

TAMINO
Sarastro herrscht in diesen Gründen?

SPRECHER
Ja! ja! Sarastro herrschet hier.

TAMINO
Doch in dem Weisheitstempel nicht?

SPRECHER
Er herrscht im Weisheitstempel hier.

TAMINO
So ist denn alles Heuchelei!

SPRECHER
Willst du schon wieder gehn?

TAMINO
Ja, ich will gehn, froh und frei,
nie euren Tempel sehn.

SPRECHER
Erklär dich näher mir,
dich täuschet ein Betrug.

but how do you expect to find this thing?
Love and Virtue do not guide you,
for Death and Vengeance goad you on.

TAMINO
Only Vengeance against the villain!

SPEAKER
Among us you will find none such.

TAMINO
Does Sarastro rule in these precincts?

SPEAKER
Oh, yes! Sarastro rules here.

TAMINO
But not in the Temple of Wisdom?

SPEAKER
He rules here in the Temple of Wisdom.

TAMINO
Then all this is hypocrisy!

SPEAKER
Do you wish to go on your way?

TAMINO
Yes, I shall go, happy and free,
never to see your Temple.

SPEAKER
Explain yourself further;
some deceit has misled you.

TAMINO

Sarastro wohnet hier?

Das ist mir schon genug.

SPRECHER

Wenn du dein Lieben liebst, so rede, bleibe
da! Sarastro hassest du?

TAMINO

Ich hass' ihn ewig, ja!

SPRECHER

So gib mir deine Gründe an.

TAMINO

Er ist ein Unmensch, ein Tyrann!

SPRECHER

Ist das, was du gesagt, erwiesen?

TAMINO

Durch ein unglücklich Weib bewiesen,
das Gram und Jammer niederdrückt.

SPRECHER

Ein Weib hat also dich berückt?
Ein Weib tut wenig, plaudert viel;
du, Jüngling, glaubst dem Zungenspiel?
O, legte doch Sarastro dir
die Absicht seiner Handlung für!

TAMINO

Die Absicht ist nur allzu klar!
Riß nicht der Räuber ohn Erbarmen
Paminen aud der Mutter Armen?

TAMINO

Sarastro resides here?

That is quite enough for me.

SPEAKER

If you value your life, say so and stay away!
Do you hate Sarastro?

TAMINO

I shall hate him forever!

SPEAKER

Give me your reasons then.

TAMINO

He is inhuman, a tyrant!

SPEAKER

Has what you say been proved?

TAMINO

It is proved by an unhappy woman,
oppressed by sorrow and pain.

SPEAKER

Has a woman so deceived you?
A woman does little, gossips much;
you, youth, believe in wagging tongues?
If only Sarastro could reveal to you
the purpose of his stratagem!

TAMINO

His purpose is all too clear!
Did not the robber snatch without pity
Pamina from her mother's arms?

SPRECHER

Ja, Jüngling, was du sagst, ist wahr.

TAMINO

Wo ist sie, die er uns geraubt?
Man opferte vielleicht sie schon?

SPRECHER

Dir dies zu sagen, teurer Sohn!
ist jetzt und mir noch nicht erlaubt.

TAMINO

Erklär dies Rätsel, täusch mich nicht!

SPRECHER

Die Zunge bindet Eid und Pflicht.

TAMINO

Wann also wird das Dunkel schwinden?

SPRECHER

Sobald dich führt der Freundschaft Hand
ins Heiligtum zum ew'gen Band.
(Geht ab.)

TAMINO

O ew'ge Nacht, wann wirst du schwinden?
Wann wird das Licht mein Auge finden?

CHOR *(von innen)*

Bald, Jüngling, oder nie!

TAMINO

Bald, sagt ihr, oder nie?
Ihr Unsichtbaren, saget mir,
lebt denn Pamina noch?

SPEAKER

Yes, young man, what you say is true.

TAMINO

Where is she whom he stole from us?
Has she perhaps already been sacrificed?

SPEAKER

To tell you this, dear son,
is not for me to say now.

TAMINO

Explain your riddle, don't deceive me!

SPEAKER

Oath and duty bind my tongue.

TAMINO

When will this pretense be cast aside?

SPEAKER

As soon as friendship's hand leads you
into the shrine for everlasting union.
(Exit.)

TAMINO

O unending night, when will you vanish?
When will my eyes see the light?

CHORUS *(from within)*

Soon, youth, or never!

TAMINO

Soon, you say, or never?
You unseen voices, tell me,
is Pamina still alive?

CHOR

Pamina lebet noch.

CHORUS

Pamina is still alive.

TAMINO

Sie lebt? sie lebt?
Ich danke euch dafür!
O! wenn ich doch im Stande wäre,
Allmächtige! zu eurer Ehre,
mit jedem Tone meinen Dank
Zu schildern, wie er hier entsprang!

TAMINO

Alive? she is alive?
I thank you for that!
Oh, if only I were able,
almighty gods, in your honour,
to express with every note
the gratitude I feel in my heart!

He plays on the magic flute; many kinds of animals and birds draw near to listen, until he stops.

TAMINO

Wie stark ist nicht dein Zauberton!
weil, holde Flöte, durch dein Spielen
selbst wilde tiere Freude fühlen.
Doch, nur Pamina bleibt davon.
Pamina, Pamina, höre mich!
Umsonst! Wo? ach! wo, wo find' ich dich?

TAMINO

How powerful is your magic music,
sweet flute, for when you play
even wild beasts feel joy!
Yet Pamina stays away.
Pamina, Pamina, hear me!
Useless! Where, ah, where shall I find you?

Papageno's pipes are heard answering in the distance.

TAMINO

Ha! das ist Papagenos Ton!
Vielleicht sah er Pamina schon,
vielleicht eilt sie mit ihm zu mir,
vielleicht führt mich der Ton zu ihr!

TAMINO

Ha! that was Papageno's call!
Perhaps he has already seen Pamina,
perhaps she hurries here with him,
perhaps the sound will lead me to her!

He goes out as Papageno and Pamina hurry in from the opposite direction.

PAMINA UND PAPAGENO

Schnelle Füße, rascher Mut
schützt vor Feindes List und Wut;

PAMINA AND PAPAGENO

Hurrying feet, ready courage
protect us from foes' craft and rage;

fänden wir Tamino doch,	if only we could find Tamino—
sonst erwischen sie uns noch!	otherwise we may be captured yet!

PAMINA (*rufend*)
Holder Jüngling!

PAMINA (*calling*)
Gentle youth!

PAPAGENO
Stille, stille, ich kann's besser!

PAPAGENO
Hush, hush, I have a better way!

Papageno plays, and Tamino replies from the distance.

PAMINA UND PAPAGENO
Welche Freude ist wohl größer!
Freund Tamino hört uns schon;
hierher kam der Flötenton!
Welch ein Glück, wenn ich ihn finde!
nur geschwinde, nur geschwinde!

PAMINA AND PAPAGENO
What joy is greater than this?
Friend Tamino has already heard us;
we heard his flute reply!
What a pleasure to find him!
So hurry on, so hurry on!

As they are about to hurry off, Monostatos suddenly bars their way, and mocks them.

MONOSTATOS
Nur geschwinde, nur geschwinde!
Ha! Hab' ich euch noch erwischt!
Nur herbei mit Stahl und Eisen!
Wart, man wird euch Mores weisen!
Den Monostatos berücken!
Nun herbei mit Band und Stricken!
He! ihr Sklaven, kommt herbei!

MONOSTATOS
So hurry on, so hurry on!
Ha! now I've captured you!
Bring here daggers and irons!
Just wait, I'll teach you manners!
To deceive Monostatos!
Bring here fetters and ropes!
Hey, you slaves, come here!

PAMINA UND PAPAGENO
Ach, nun ist's mit uns vorbei!

PAMINA AND PAPAGENO
Ah, now we're done for!

PAPAGENO
Wer viel wagt, gewinnt oft viel!
Komm, du schönes Glockenspiel,

PAPAGENO
He who ventures much has much to gain!
Come, my pretty chest of bells,

laß die Glöckchen klingen, klingen,
daß die Ohren ihnen singen.

let your bells ring and ring
and make their ears sing!

Papageno plays on his bells, and the Slaves who have run out at Monostatos's command join him in a dance.

MONOSTATOS UND DIE SKLAVEN
Das klinget so herrlich, das klinget so schön!
La-ra-la, la la la-ra-la!
Nie hab' ich so etwas gehört und gesehn!
La-ra-la, la la la-ra-la!

MONOSTATOS AND THE SLAVES
That sounds so pretty, that sounds so fine!
La-ra-la, la la la-ra-la!
Never did I hear and see anything like that!
La-ra-la, la la la-ra-la!

They withdraw, singing and dancing.

PAMINA UND PAPAGENO
Könnte jeder brave Mann
solche Glöckchen finden,
seine Feinde würden dann
ohne Mühe schwinden;
und er lebte ohne sie
in der besten Harmonie.
Nur der Freundschaft Harmonie
mildert die Beschwerden,
ohne diese Sympathie
ist kein Glück auf Erden.

PAMINA AND PAPAGENO
If every honest man
could find such bells,
his enemies would then
easily disappear;
he would live free of them
in perfect harmony.
Only the harmony of friendship
eases all hardships,
and without this sympathy
there is no joy on earth.

CHOR *(von innen)*
Es lebe Sarastro, Sarastro lebe!

CHORUS *(from within)*
Long live Sarastro—Sarastro, all hail!

PAPAGENO
Was soll das bedeuten? Ich zittre, ich bebe!

PAPAGENO
What can that mean? I shiver and shake!

PAMINA
O! Freund, nun ist's um uns getan;
dies kündigt den Sarastro an!

PAMINA
Oh, my friend, now we're finished;
this announces Sarastro's approach!

PAPAGENO

O wär ich eine Maus,
wie wollt' ich mich verstecken!
Wär ich so klein wie Schnecken,
so kröch' ich in mein Haus!
Mein Kind, was werden wir nun sprechen?

PAMINA

Die Wahrheit! wär sie auch Verbrechen!

Enter Sarastro and his retinue.

CHOR

Es lebe Sarastro, Sarastro soll leben!
Er ist es, dem wir uns mit Freuden ergeben!
Stets mög er des Lebens als Weiser sich
freun!
Er ist unser Abgott, dem alle sich weihn!

PAMINA *kniend*

Herr! Ich bin zwar Verbrecherin!
Ich wollte deiner Macht entfliehn.
Allein, die Schuld liegt nicht an mir
Der böse Mohr verlangte Liebe,
darum, o Herr! entfloh ich dir.

SARASTRO

Steh auf, erheitre dich, o Liebe!
denn ohne erst in dich zu dringen,
weiß ich von deinem Herzen mehr;
du liebest einen andern sehr.
Zur Liebe will ich dich nicht zwingen,
doch geb' ich dir die Freiheit nicht.

PAPAGENO

If only I were a mouse—
how I'd hide myself!
If only I were tiny as a snail
I'd creep into my house!
My child, what will we say now?

PAMINA

The truth—even if that were a crime!

CHORUS

Long live Sarastro—Sarastro, all hail!
To him we consecrate ourselves with joy!
May he ever, in his wisdom, take pleasure
in life! He is the idol to whom we dedicate
ourselves!

PAMINA *kneeling*

My lord! I am the transgressor!
I wished to escape your power.
Yet the guilt is not my own
the wicked Moor demanded love—
and therefore, my lord, I ran away.

SARASTRO

Arise, be cheerful, my beloved!
For without probing I know
more from your very own heart;
you love another very deeply.
I will not force you to love,
yet I will not grant your freedom.

PAMINA

Mich rufet ja die Kindespflicht,
denn meine Mutter —

SARASTRO

Steht in meiner Macht;
du würdest um dein Glück gebracht,
wenn ich dich ihren Händen ließe.

PAMINA

Mir klingt der Muttername süße!
Sie ist es, sie ist es —

SARASTRO

Und ein stolzes Weib!
Ein Mann muß eure Herzen leiten
denn ohne ihn pflegt jedes Weib
aus ihrem Wirkungskreis schreiten.

Monostatos enters with Tamino.

MONOSTATOS

Du stolzer Jüngling, nur hierher!
Hier ist Sarastro, unser Herr.

PAMINA

Er ist's!

TAMINO

Sie ist's!

PAMINA

Ich glaub' es kaum!

TAMINO

Es ist kein Traum!

PAMINA

The duty of a child summons me,
for my mother—

SARASTRO

Lies in my power;
your happiness would be forever destroyed
If I delivered you into her hands.

PAMINA

To me my mother's name sounds sweet!
It is she, it is she—

SARASTRO

She is an arrogant woman!
A man must guide your heart,
for without that, every woman tends to
overstep her natural sphere.

MONOSTATOS

Now, proud youth, come here!
Here is Sarastro, our master.

PAMINA

It is he!

TAMINO

It is she!

PAMINA

I can hardly believe it!

TAMINO

This is not a dream!

PAMINA UND TAMINO

Es schling' mein Arm sich um ihn (sie) her.
und wenn es auch mein Ende wär!

They embrace.

CHOR

Was soll das heißen?

MONOSTATOS

Welch eine Dreistigkeit!
Gleich auseinander, das geht zu weit!

Monostatos separates them; kneeling before Sarastro:

Dein Sklave liegt zu deinen Füßen,
laß den verwegnen Frevler büßen!
Bedenk, wie frech der Knabe ist!
Durch dieses seltnen Vogels List
wollt er Pamina dir entführen,
allein ich wußt' ihn aufzuspüren.
Du kennst mich, meine Wachsamkeit —

SARASTRO

Verdient, daß man ihr Lorbeer streut!
He! gebt dem Ehrenmann sogleich —

MONOSTATOS

Schon deine Gnade macht mich reich!

SARASTRO

— Nur sieben und siebenzig
Sohlenstreich'!

MONOSTATOS

Ach, Herr! den Lohn verhofft' ich nicht!

PAMINA AND TAMINO

My arms will embrace him (her)
even if that means my death!

CHORUS

Whatever may this be?

MONOSTATOS

What impertinence!
Get away from each other, you go too far!

Your slave lies at your feet
let the foolhardy sinner be punished!
Think how brazen the boy is!
Through the cunning of this peculiar bird
he meant to steal away Pamina,
and I alone knew how to track him down.
You know me, my vigilance—

SARASTRO

It deserves a path of laurel leaves!
Ho! give unto the worthy man—

MONOSTATOS

Your favour already makes me rich!

SARASTRO

—Seventy-seven liar's
blows!

MONOSTATOS

Ah, sir! for such payment I hardly hoped!

SARASTRO

Nicht Dank! es ist ja meine Pflicht!

Monostatos is led away by some Slaves.

CHOR

Es lebe Sarastro, der göttliche Weise!
er lohnet und strafet in ähnlichem Kreise.

SARASTRO

Führt diese beiden Fremdlinge
in unsern Prüfungstempel ein;
bedecket ihre Häupter dann,
sie müssen erst gereinigt sein.

CHOR

Wenn Tugend und Gerechtigkeit
den Großen Pfad mit Ruhm bestreut,
dann ist die Erd' ein Himmelreich,
und Sterbliche den Göttern gleich.

SARASTRO

Do not thank me! It is my duty!

CHORUS

Long live Sarastro, the godly-wise!
He rewards and punishes in equal degree.

SARASTRO

Take both of these strangers
into the temple of trial;
then cover their heads,
for they must first be purified.

CHORUS

If virtue and righteousness
pave the Great Path with renown,
then the earth will be a heavenly kingdom
and mortals will be like the gods.

Act 2

DISC NO. 1/TRACK 16

March of the Priests Touching in its gentle reverence, the processional opening the second act suggests that the madcap twists and turns of the first act have been left behind. Brief but noble, it was played at the Metropolitan Opera one evening in 1962, upon the announcement of the death of Bruno Walter, the great Mozart conductor and interpreter of this opera.

A palm grove.

Entrance of Sarastro and other priests in solemn procession.

SCENE NINE
March of the Priests

DISC NO. 1/TRACK 17

Ihr in den Weisheitstempel eingeweihten Diener. The stately dialogue between Sarastro and his Speaker continues the sense of calm dignity expressed in the March.

SARASTRO

Ihr in den Weisheitstempel
eingeweihten Diener der großen Göttin
Osiris und Isis, ich erkläre euch, daß unsere
heutige Versammlung von großer
Bedeutung ist — Tamino, ein Königssohn,
wandelt an der nördlichen Pforte unseres
Tempels. Er will den nächtlichen Schleier
von sich reißen und ins Heiligtum des
größten Lichtes blicken, ihm freund-
schaftlich die Hand zu bieten, sei heute
eine unserer wichtigsten Pflichten.

SARASTRO

You servants of the great gods Osiris and
Isis, consecrated in the Temple of Wisdom,
I declare unto you that our assembly today
is of the greatest importance. Tamino, a
king's son, is waiting at the north door of
our Temple. He wants to tear off from
himself the veil of night and look into
the sanctuary of the supreme light.
To offer him the hand of friendship
shall be one of our most important
duties today.

ERSTER PRIESTER
Er besitzt Tugend?

SARASTRO
Tugend.

SPRECHER
Auch Verschwiegenheit?

SARASTRO
Verschwiegenheit.

ERSTER PRIESTER
Ist wohltätig?

SARASTRO
Wohltätig. Haltet ihn für würdig,
so folgt meinem Beispiel.

They sound their trumpets.

Pamina, das tugendhafte Mädchen, haben
die Götter dem Jüngling bestimmt; dies ist
der Grund, warum ich sie der stolzen
Mutter entriß, —
das Weib dünkt sich groß zu sein und
versucht, unsern festen Tempelbau zu
zerstören.Das soll sie nicht. Tamino selbst
soll ihn mit uns befestigen.

They sound their trumpets.

SPRECHER
Großer Sarastro, wird Tamino auch

FIRST PRIEST
Does he possess virtue?

SARASTRO
Virtue.

SPEAKER
And reticence?

SARASTRO
Reticence.

FIRST PRIEST
And is full of good deeds?

SARASTRO
Good deeds.
If you think he is worthy, then follow my
example.

Pamina, that virtuous girl, has been chosen
by the gods for this gentle youth; that is
the reason why I remove her from her
proud mother. That woman fancies herself
to be important and is trying to destroy the
solid fabric of our Temple. But she shall
not! Tamino himself shall join us in
strengthening it.

SPEAKER
Great Sarastro, will Tamino also withstand

die schweren Prüfungen bestehen? — Er ist Prinz!	the severe trials that await him? Remember, he is a prince!

SARASTRO

Mehr noch — er ist Mensch!

SARASTRO

Even more he is a human being!

SPRECHER

Wenn er aber im harten Kampfe unterliegt?

SPEAKER

But what if he is killed in the fight?

SARASTRO

Dann wird er der Götter Freunden früher fühlen als wir.

SARASTRO

Then he will experience the joys of the gods sooner than we!

They sound trumpets.

Man führe Tamino mit seinem Reisegefährten in den Vorhof des Tempels! Und ihr, Freunde, vollziehet euer heiliges Amt und lehret die beiden die Weisheit und Macht der Götter erkennen!

Let Tamino and his companion be led into the forecourt of the Temple! And you, my friends, fulfill your sacred office and teach the two of them to acknowledge the wisdom and power of the gods.

DISC NO. 1/TRACK 18

O Isis und Osiris **This prayer for the deliverance of Papageno and Tamino as they endure the rituals of initiation into the brotherhood is one of the most moving passages in the score. Mozart exploits the bass voice in all its resonant depth and majesty (01:04), and the echoing of the men's chorus (01:18), at the end of each of Sarastro's thoughts, has an unearthly effect.**

Hans Sotin, German bass, as Sarastro, his most famous role.

SCENE TEN
Aria and Chorus

SARASTRO

O Isis und Osiris, schenket
der Weisheit Geist dem neuen Paar!
Die ihr der Wandrer Schritte lenket,
stärkt mit Geduld sie in Gefahr!

CHOR

Stärkt mit Geduld sie in Gefahr!

SARASTRO

Laßt sie der Prüfung Früchte sehen;
doch sollten sie zu Grabe gehen,
so lohnt der Tugend kühnen Lauf,
nehmt sie in euren Wohnsitz auf!

CHOR

Nehmt sie in euren Wohnsitz auf!

SARASTRO

O Isis and Osiris, grant
the spirit of wisdom to the new pair!
You that guide the steps of wanderers,
strengthen them in danger!

CHORUS

Strengthen them in danger!

SARASTRO

Let them see the fruits of their trial;
but if they should go to their grave,
reward the bold course of their virtue
and take them up into your dwelling place.

CHORUS

Take them up into your dwelling place.

Exit Sarastro, followed by all the others.

The scene changes to the forecourt of the Temple. It is night. Thunder is heard rumbling in the distance.

Tamino and Papageno are led in by two priests, who then depart.

> **DISC NO. 2/TRACK 1**

Eine schreckliche Nacht. **The imposing Priests question Tamino and Papageno.**

TAMINO

Eine schreckliche Nacht. —
Papageno, bist du noch bei mir?

TAMINO

What a terrible night!
Papageno, are you still with me?

PAPAGENO

Ja, leider

(Donnerschlag)

O weh! O weh!

TAMINO

Du hast Furcht?

PAPAGENO

F . . . Furcht, Furcht eben nicht,
nur, es läuft mir so eiskalt über den
Rücken.

(Donnerschlag)

O weh! O . . .

TAMINO

Papageno, sei ein Mann!

PAPAGENO

Ich wollt', ich wär' ein Mädchen!

(Donnerschlag)

Oh! D . . . das ist mein letzer Augenblick!

Two priests enter carrying torches.

ZWEITER PRIESTER

Ihr Fremdlinge, was sucht
ihr? Was treibt euch an, in unsre Mauern
zu dringen?

TAMINO

Freundschaft und Liebe!

ZWEITER PRIESTER

Bist du bereit, sie mit
deinem Leben zu erkämpfen?

PAPAGENO

I'm afraid so.

(Clap of thunder)

Oh dear, oh dear!

TAMINO

Are you frightened?

PAPAGENO

F-frightened? Not frightened exactly, it's
just that shivers are running down my
spine.

(Clap of thunder)

Oh dear!

TAMINO

Papageno, be a man!

PAPAGENO

I wish I were a girl!

(Clap of thunder)

Oh, no, my last moment has come!

SECOND PRIEST

You strangers, what do you want? What
has possessed you to penetrate within our
walls?

TAMINO

Friendship and love.

SECOND PRIEST

Are you prepared to stake your life in
fighting to acquire them?

TAMINO

Ja! Weisheitslehre sei mein Sieg;
Pamina mein Lohn!

ZWEITER PRIESTER

Reiche mir deine Hand! —
Du wirst Pamina sehen, sie aber nicht
sprechen dürfen; das ist der Anfang deiner
Prüfung.

ERSTER PRIESTER

Papageno!

PAPAGENO

Hm.

ERSTER PRIESTER

Willst auch du die
Weisheitslehre erkämpfen?

PAPAGENO

Na . . . , kämpfen ist mein Sache nicht.
i . . . ich bin so ein Naturmensch, der sich
mitis Schlaf, Speise und Trank begnügt; und
wenn es mal sein könnte, daß ich mir ein
schönes Weibchen fange . . .

ERSTER PRIESTER

Das wirst du nie erhalten, wenn du dich
nicht unseren Prüfungen unterziehst
und selbst den Tod nicht scheust!

PAPAGENO

Ich bleibe ledig!

TAMINO

Yes! May the knowledge of wisdom be my
victory, and Pamina my reward!

SECOND PRIEST

Give me your hand. You will see Pamina,
but you will not be permitted to speak to
her. That is the beginning of
your trials.

FIRST PRIEST

Papageno!

PAPAGENO

Hm?

FIRST PRIEST

Are you, too, willing to gain the knowledge
of wisdom by fighting for it?

PAPAGENO

Well . . . fighting isn't really my line; nor
is wisdom, come to that, I'm a simple soul,
satisfied with sleep, food and drink; and
maybe if I could catch a beautiful
woman . . .

FIRST PRIEST

You will never get one if you don't undergo
our trials, fearless in the face of
death.

PAPAGENO

I'll stay single!

ERSTER PRIESTER

Wenn nun aber Sarastro
für dich ein Mädchen hätte, das an Farbe
und Kleidung dir ganz gleich wäre . . .

PAPAGENO

Mir ganz gleicht? Hört!
Mir ganz gleicht? Ist sie jung?

ERSTER PRIESTER

Sehr jung!

PAPAGENO

Hmm . . .

ERSTER PRIESTER

Und heißt Papagena.

PAPAGENO

Pa . . . wie? wie? Papage . . .

ERSTER PRIESTER

. . . na!

PAPAGENO

Na? Ah, Papagena. Die möchte ich
aus bloßer Neugierde sehen?

ERSTER PRIESTER

Sehen kannst du sie, aber
kein Wort mit ihr sprechen! Wird dein
Geist soviel Standhaftigkeit besitzen?

PAPAGENO

O ja!

FIRST PRIEST

But suppose Sarastro had a girl waiting for
you, just like you in
colours and clothing?

PAPAGENO

Just like me? I say! Just like me? Is she
young?

FIRST PRIEST

Very young.

PAPAGENO

Mmm . . .

FIRST PRIEST

And she's called Papagena.

PAPAGENO

Pa . . . what? Eh? Papage . . .

FIRST PRIEST

. . . na!

PAPAGENO

Na? Oh, I see, Papagena. I'd like to see her
out of sheer curiosity!

FIRST PRIEST

You may see her, but not speak a single
word to her. Will you be able to summon
up so much steadfastness of purpose?

PAPAGENO

Oh, yes!

Bewahret euch vor Weibertücken. **The Priests warn Tamino and Papageno against women's wiles in stern and formal music.**

SCENE ELEVEN
Duet

ZWEI PRIESTER

Bewahret euch vor Weibertücken
dies ist des Bundes erste Pflicht!
Manch weiser Mann ließ sich berücken,
er fehlte und versah sich's nicht;
verlassen sah er sich am Ende,
vergolten seine Treu' mit Hohn!
Vergebens rang er seine Hände,
Tod und Verzweiflung war sein Lohn.

TWO PRIESTS

Guard yourself from women's tricks
this is the first duty of our order!
Many a wise man has been deceived,
has failed and never seen his error;
he found himself finally abandoned,
His faithfulness paid back with scorn!
In vain were all his struggles,
for death and despair were his reward.

The Two Priests go out.

PAPAGENO

He, Lichter her! Das ist doch
wunderlich, sooft einen die Herren verlassen,
sieht man mit offenen Augen nichts.

PAPAGENO

Hey, let's have some light!
It's quite extraordinary
as often as these gentlemen leave you,
you're plunged into darkness.

TAMINO

Ertrag es mit Geduld und denk,
es ist der Götter Wille.

TAMINO

Bear it with patience and accept it as the
will of the gods.

Tamino and Papageno remind themselves that true love awaits them if they face their trials bravely.

Duet

TAMINO Pamina, wo bist du?	**TAMINO** Pamina, where are you?
PAPAGENO Ach Weibchen, wo bist du?	**PAPAGENO** My girl, where are you?
TAMINO UND PAPAGENO Getrennt von dir zu ein, ist mir die größte Pein.	**TAMINO AND PAPAGENO** To be parted from you pains me more than anything.
TAMINO Schaff meinem Herzen Ruh'!	**TAMINO** Ease my heartache.
PAPAGENO Ach Weibchen, wo bist du?	**PAPAGENO** My girl, where are you?
TAMINO Pamina! Pamina! Pamina! Nur sehen will ich dich und fragen Liebst du mich? Dann tret' ich kühn die Bahn zum neuen Leben an. Nun zur Pamina . . .	**TAMINO** Pamina, Pamina, Pamina! I only want to see you and ask you, "Do you love me?" Then I will boldly step forth to a new life. Now to Pamina . . .
PAPAGENO . . . und Papagena!	**PAPAGENO** . . . and Papagena!
TAMINO UND PAPAGENO Stille, stille, stille, stille.	**TAMINO AND PAPAGENO** Softly, softly, softly, softly.

The Three Ladies appear.

DISC NO. 2/TRACKS 5 & 6

Wie? wie? wie? ihr an diesem Schreckensort? **The Three Ladies are back, trembling with fear because the Queen of the Night is breathing fire. Their appearance could not be more inap-**

propriate, and Mozart has some fun here at their expense. Though they are terrified, the music makes fun of them and plays up their ineptitude (00:53). The angry offstage response of the priests (02:39) suggests that the purity of the ritual has been breached, but the three-fold chord (heard at the beginning of Track No. 6) assures that all is well.

SCENE TWELVE
Quintet

DIE DAMEN

Wie? wie? wie? ihr an diesem
Schreckensort?
Nie, nie, nie, kommt ihr glücklich
wieder fort!
Tamino, dir ist Tod geschworen;
du Papageno, bist verloren!

PAPAGENO

Nein, nein, nein, das wär' zu viel!

TAMINO

Papageno, schweige still!
Willst due dein Gelübde brechen,
nichts mit Weibern hier zu sprechen?

PAPAGENO

Du hörst ja, wir sind beide hin.

TAMINO

Stille, sag' ich, schweige still!

PAPAGENO

Immer still und immer still!

DIE DAMEN

Ganz nah ist euch die Königin,
sie drang im Tempel heimlich ein.

THE LADIES

What? What? What? you in this frightful
place?
Never, never, never will you have the
fortune to escape!
Tamino, death is sworn for you;
you, Papageno, are lost!

PAPAGENO

No, no, no, that would be too much!

TAMINO

Papageno, be quiet!
Will you break your vows
by speaking idly with these women?

PAPAGENO

You heard them, we are done for.

TAMINO

Quiet, I say, be quiet!

PAPAGENO

Always quiet, always quiet!

THE LADIES

The Queen is near by you here,
she has secretly entered the temple.

PAPAGENO
Wie, was? sie soll im Tempel sein?

TAMINO
Stille, sag' ich! schweige still!
Wirst du immer so vermessen
deiner Eidespflicht vergessen?

DIE DAMEN
Tamino, hör, du bist verloren!
Gedenke an die Königin!
Man zischelt viel sich in die Ohren
von dieser Priester falschem Sinn.

TAMINO *(für sich)*
Ein Weiser prüft und achtet nicht,
was der gemeine Pöbel spricht.

DIE DAMEN
Man sagt, wer ihrem Bunde schwört,
der fährt zur Höll, mit Haupt und Haar.

PAPAGENO
Das wär' beim Teufel underhört!
Sag an, Tamino, ist das wahr?

TAMINO
Geschwätz von Weibern nachgesagt,
von Heuchlern aber ausgedacht.

PAPAGENO
Doch sagt es auch die Königin.

TAMINO
Sie ist ein Weib, hat Weibersinn.

PAPAGENO
How's that? She is in the temple?

TAMINO
Quiet, I say, be quiet!
Will you always presume
to forget your sworn duty?

THE LADIES
Tamino, listen, you are lost!
Think of the Queen!
Much is whispered concerning
the wicked ways of these priests.

TAMINO *(to himself)*
A wise man seeks proof, disregards
what the common rabble say.

THE LADIES
They say that whoever joins their league
goes straight to Hell, with hair and hide.

PAPAGENO
Enough to frighten the Devil!
Tell me, Tamino, is that true?

TAMINO
Gossip passed among womenfolk,
but invented by hypocrites.

PAPAGENO
Yet the Queen says so too.

TAMINO
She is a woman, with a woman's mind.

Sei still, mein Wort sei dir genug
denk deiner Pflicht und handle klug!

DIE DAMEN *(zu Tamino)*
Warum bist du mit uns so spröde?
Auch Papageno schweigt? so rede!

PAPAGENO
Ich möchte gerne . . . wohl . . .

TAMINO
Still!

PAPAGENO
Ihr seht, daß ich nicht soll!
Daß ich nicht kann das Plaudern lassen,
ist wahrlich eine Schand' für mich.

TAMINO
Still! Daß du nicht kannst das Plaudern
lassen, ist wahrlich eine Schand' für dich.

DIE DAMEN
Wir müssen sie mit Scham verlassen,
es plaudert keiner sicherlich.

TAMINO UND PAPAGENO
Sie müssen uns mit Scham verlassen,
es plaudert keiner sicherlich.

ALLE
Von festem Geiste ist ein Mann,
er denket, was er sprechen kann.

Be quiet, let my word be enough;
remember our duty and stay on guard!

THE LADIES *(to Tamino)*
Why are you so sharp with us?
Papageno too is silent? Speak!

PAPAGENO
Gladly I . . . would . . .

TAMINO
Hush!

PAPAGENO
You see that I may not!
That I cannot give up chattering
is truly a hardship for me.

TAMINO
Hush! That you cannot give up chattering
is truly a hardship for you.

THE LADIES
In shame we have to leave you,
neither of you will say a word.

TAMINO AND PAPAGENO
In shame you have to leave us,
neither of us will say a word.

ALL
A man is strong in spirit;
he considers of what he may speak.

The Three Ladies are just about to go, when from within the Temple the initiates cry:

CHOR (von innen)

Entweiht ist die heilige Schwelle,

hinab mit den Weibern zur Hölle!

DIE DAMEN

O weh! o weh!

PAPAGENO

O weh! o weh!

The Two Priests enter, carrying torches.

ZWEITER PRIESTER

Tamino! Dein standhaft
männliches Betragen hat gesiegt. Wir
wollen nun unsere Wanderschaft fortsetzen.

Tamino is led away by the second priest.

ERSTER PRIESTER

Was seh' ich, Freund,
steh auf! Wie ist dir?

PAPAGENO

Scht! Ich lieg' in einer Ohnmacht!

ERSTER PRIESTER

Auf, sammle dich!

PAPAGENO (steht auf)

Aber sagt mir nur,
meine Herren, wenn mir die Götter eine
Papagena bestimmt haben, warum sie
unter soviel Mühen und Qualen erringen?

CHORUS (from within)

The sacred threshold is defiled,

away with the women to Hell!

THE LADIES

Oh, woe! woe!

PAPAGENO

Oh, woe! woe!

SECOND PRIEST

Tamino! Your manly steadfastness has
prevailed. Let us continue our journey.

FIRST PRIEST

What do I see?
Stand up, my friend; how are you feeling?

PAPAGENO

Sssh! I've fainted.

FIRST PRIEST

Get up, pull yourself together!

PAPAGENO (gets up)

But tell me one thing, gentlemen, if the
gods are providing me with a Papagena,
why do I have to go through all this agony
and torment to get her?

ERSTER PRIESTER	FIRST PRIEST

ERSTER PRIESTER

Diese neugierige Frage mag
dir deine Vernunft beantworten.

FIRST PRIEST

No doubt your intelligence will be able to
answer that inquisitive question.

PAPAGENO

O je!

PAPAGENO

Oh dear!

ERSTER PRIESTER

Komm jetzt!

FIRST PRIEST

Now, come along.

PAPAGENO

Bei so einer ewigen Wanderschaft
möcht' einem die Liebe auf immer
vergehn.

PAPAGENO

On a never-ending tramp like this you
could really lose all desire for love for the
rest of your life!

Papageno is led away by the first priest. The scene changes to a garden.

*In a bower of flowers and roses Pamina is seen to be sleeping in the light of the full moon. Monostatos
enters stealthily.*

MONOSTATOS

Ha! Da find' ich ja die spröde
Schöne! Welcher Mensch würde bei so
einem Anblick kalt und unempfindlich
bleiben? Wenn ich wüßte, daß ich so ganz
allein und unbelauscht wäre — ein
Küßchen, dächte ich, ließe sich
entschuldigen.

MONOSTATOS

Ah, now I've found you, my prim little
beauty! Who could remain cold and
unmoved at such a sight? If I could be sure
I was quite alone and unobserved, I think
a little kiss might well be excused.

DISC NO. 2/TRACK 7

Alles fühlt der Liebe Freuden Monostatos is a nasty little man, and Mozart superbly delineates
his character in this jot of an aria that flutters with impotent rage. The touch is light, and
the orchestra almost never rises above piano. Monostatos, longing for a woman (00:51), has

the opposite affect of Papageno; whereas Papageno sounds virile and easily aroused, Monostatos sounds impotent and merely annoying.

SCENE THIRTEEN
Aria

MONOSTATOS

Alles fühlt der Liebe Freuden,
schnäbelt, tändelt, herzet, küßt,
und ich soll die Liebe meiden,
weil ein Schwarzer häßlich ist!
Ist mir denn kein Herz gegeben?
Bin ich nicht von Fleisch und Blut?
Immer ohne Weibchen leben
wäre wahrlich Höllenglut!
Drum so will ich, weil ich lebe,
schnäbeln, küssen, zärtlich sein!
Lieber guter Mond, vergebe
eine Weiße nahm mich ein.
Weiß ist schön, ich muß sie küssen
Mond, verstecke dich dazu!
Sollt' es dich zu sehr verdrießen,
o so mach die Augen zu!

MONOSTATOS

Every creature feels love's joys,
nuzzles, dallies, hugs and kisses,
but I must shun love
because a black man is ugly!
Was I not given a heart?
Am I not made of flesh and blood?
To live forever without a wife
would be sheer hell-fire!
And so will I, while I live,
nuzzle, kiss, be amorous!
Beloved moon, forgive me
I was taken by a white skin.
White is beautiful, I must kiss her
Moon, hide yourself from me!
If it gives you too much grief,
then you must close your eyes!

He steals forward towards Pamina.

KÖNIGIN

appearing

Zurück!

MONOSTATOS
O weh! Die Königin der Nacht!

QUEEN

Get back!

MONOSTATOS
Oh dear, the Queen of the Night!

Mutter! Meine Mutter! **The Queen of the Night returns in a fury in a hysterical aria that makes her earlier one sound thoughtful by comparison. She is virtually howling in rage (track 9, 00:27), transformed by Mozart into a spine-tingling coloratura (00:40). In a performance such as Edda Moser's on this recording, the effect is shattering in its tightly wound intensity.**

PAMINA

wakening

Mutter! Meine Mutter!

MONOSTATOS
Mutter? Das muß man von
weitem belauschen!

He hides.

KÖNIGIN
Wo ist der Jüngling, den ich zu dir sandte?

PAMINA
Er hat sich den Eingeweihten gewidmet!

KÖNIGIN
Den Eingeweihten? Unglückliche
Tochter! Nun bist du mir auf ewig
entrissen —
Nimm hier diesen Dolch! Er ist für
Sarastro geschliffen. Du wirst ihn töten
und den mächtigen
Sonnenkreis mir überliefern!

PAMINA
Aber liebste Mutter!

PAMINA

Mother, Mother!

MONOSTATOS
Mother? I must eavesdrop
on this!

QUEEN
Where is the young man I sent to you?

PAMINA
He has joined the initiates!

QUEEN
The initiates? Unhappy daughter!
Now you will be taken from me forever!
Here, take this dagger. It has been
sharpened for Sarastro.
You are to kill him and bring me the
powerful solar orb he wears on his breast.

PAMINA
But dearest Mother!

KÖNIGIN	QUEEN
Kein Wort!	Not a word!

SCENE FOURTEEN
Aria

KÖNIGIN

Der Hölle Rache kocht in meinem Herzen;
Tod und Verzweiflung flammet um mich
her! Fühlt nicht durch dich Sarastro
Todesschmerzen, so bist du meine Tochter
nimmermehr! Verstoßen sei auf ewig, verlassen sei auf ewig, zertrümmert sei auf
ewig alle Bande der Natur — wenn nicht
durch dich Sarastro wird erblassen! Hört!
Rachengötter! Hört der Mutter Schwur!

QUEEN

The vengeance of Hell boils in my heart;
death and despair flame around me!
If you do not cause Sarastro a painful death
you will be my daughter no more!
Outcast forever, abandoned forever,
destroyed forever be all ties of nature—
if Sarastro does not die through you!
Hear me, gods of vengeance! Hear a
mother's vow!

The Queen of the Night vanishes again.

Cristina Deutekom as the Queen of the
Night, the role in which she made her
1967 debut at the Metropolitan Opera.

Morden soll ich? **Pamina's problems keep mounting as the horrible Monostatos returns again.**

PAMINA *(mit dem Dolch in der Hand)*
Morden soll ich? — Das kann ich nicht!
Das kann ich nicht! O Götter, was soll ich
tun?

PAMINA *(with the dagger in her hand)*
Me murder? I cannot, I cannot!
O gods,
what shall I do?

MONASTATOS *(kommt hervor)*
Dich mir anvertrauen!

MONOSTATOS *(coming forward)*
Entrust yourself to me!

PAMINA *(erschreckt)*
Ha!

PAMINA *(starting with fright)*
Oh!

MONOSTATOS
Warum zitterst du?
Vor meiner schwarzen Farbe, oder vor dem
geplanten Mord?!

MONOSTATOS
What are you trembling for?
At my black skin, or at the murder
plan?

PAMINA
Du weißt also?

PAMINA
So you know?

MONOSTATOS
Alles! Du hast nur einen Weg,
dich und deine Mutter zu retten.

MONOSTATOS
Everything! There is only one way you can
save yourself and your mother.

PAMINA
Und der wäre?

PAMINA
And that is?

MONOSTATOS
Mich zu lieben.

MONOSTATOS
By loving me!

PAMINA
Nein!

PAMINA
Never!

MONOSTATOS	**MONOSTATOS**
So stirb!	Then die!
SARASTRO	**SARASTRO**
appearing	
Zurück!	Get back!
MONOSTATOS	**MONOSTATOS**
Herr, ich bin unschuldig.	Lord, I am innocent.
SARASTRO	**SARASTRO**
Geh!	Away with you!
MONOSTATOS *(leise)*	**MONOSTATOS** *(aside)*
Jetzt such' ich die Mutter auf.	Now I'll go and find her mother.
Steals away.	
PAMINA	**PAMINA**
Herr, strafe meine Mutter nicht!	Lord, do not punish my mother!
Der Schmerz über meine Abwesenheit . . .	The pain of my absence . . .
SARASTRO	**SARASTRO**
Ich weiß alles, allein, du sollst sehen,	I know all. But you shall see how I will
wie ich mich an deiner Mutter räche.	take vengeance on your mother.

DISC NO. 2/TRACK 11

In diesen heil'gen Hallen As if to further indicate the corrosive effect of the Queen of the
Night, Mozart follows her outburst with another beautifully reflective aria for Sarastro. In
a melody of paternal warmth and reassurance, Sarastro tells Pamina that he and his followers have the best and most honorable intentions. They will not sink to the vicious level of
the queen in vanquishing her.

SCENE FIFTEEN
Aria

SARASTRO

In diesen heil'gen Hallen
kennt man die Rache nicht,
und ist ein Mensch gefallen,
führt Liebe ihn zur Pflicht.
Dann wandelt er an Freundes Hand,
vergnügt und froh ins bessre Land.
In diesen heil'gen Mauern,
wo Mensch den Menschen liebt,
kann kein Verräter lauern,
weil man dem Feind vergibt.
Wen solche Lehren nicht erfreun,
verdienet nicht, ein Mensch zu sein.

SARASTRO

In these sacred halls
we know no revenge,
and when a man has fallen,
love comes to his aid.
Then a friend's hand guides him
satisfied, happy, to a better land.
Within these sacred walls,
where mankind loves mankind,
there lurks no betrayer,
for we forgive our enemies.
Who is not pleased by such teaching
is not worthy to be called man.

Exeunt.

The scene changes to a hall.

Tamino and Papageno are led in by the Two Priests.

DISC NO. 2/TRACK 12

Hier seid ihr beide euch allein überlassen **Despite the stern warnings from the Priests, Papageno cannot keep his vows very long and soon (00:46) is chatting with a flirty old lady.**

ZWEITER PRIESTER

Hier seid ihr beide euch
allein überlassen; Prinz, — noch einmal,
vergeßt nicht: schweigen!

SECOND PRIEST

Here you will be left to yourselves. You,
Prince, once again, do not forget: keep
silent!

ERSTER PRIESTER

Papageno!

FIRST PRIEST

Papageno!

PAPAGENO

Hm.

ERSTER PRIESTER

Wer an diesem Ort sein
Stillschweigen bricht, den strafen die
Götter durch Donner und Blitz. Leb wohl!

PAPAGENO

Leb wohl! Auf Wiedersehen!
Lustig! Das ist ein lustiges Leben. — Wär'
ich doch lieber in meiner Strohhütte im
Wald geblieben, da hört' ich doch wenig-
stens manchmal einen Vogel pfeifen.

TAMINO

Ssst!

PAPAGENO

Mit mir werd' ich noch sprechen
dürfen, wir zwei können auch miteinander
reden, weil wir sind ja Männer!

TAMINO

Ssst!

PAPAGENO

Lalalala . . .

TAMINO

Sst!

PAPAGENO

Lalala . . .

PAPAGENO

Mm?

FIRST PRIEST

He who breaks his vow of silence here will
be punished by the gods with thunder and
lightning. Farewell!

PAPAGENO

Farewell! Adieu!
It's a funny life.
If only I had stayed in my straw hut back
in the forest, at least I would hear a bird
singing occasionally.

TAMINO

Ssh!

PAPAGENO

Surely I'm allowed to talk to myself?
And we can talk to each other, too, because
we are men.

TAMINO

Ssh!

PAPAGENO

Lalalala . . .

TAMINO

Ssh!

PAPAGENO

Lalala . . .

TAMINO

Sst!

PAPAGENO

Lalala! — Nicht einmal einen Tropfen Wasser bekommt man bei diesen Leuten.

Enter an ugly old crone with a large goblet of water.

WEIB *(lachend)*

Hier, mein Engel!

PAPAGENO

Ist der Becher für mich?

WEIB

Freilich, mein Engel, freilich!

PAPAGENO *(trinkt einen Schluck)*

Ha! Brrr! Wasser! — Komm, Alte, setz dich her zu mir, sag einmal, wie alt bist du denn?

WEIB

Achtzehn Jahr' und zwei Minuten.

PAPAGENO

Achtzig Jahr' und zwei Minuten.

WEIB

Achtzehn Jahr' und zwei Minuten.

PAPAGENO

Hahaha! Achtzehn! Haha! Ei, du junger Engel! Du, du, hast du auch einen Geliebten?

TAMINO

Ssh!

PAPAGENO

Lalala . . . You don't even get a drop of water from the people round here.

CRONE *(laughing)*

Here you are, my angel.

PAPAGENO

Is that for me?

CRONE

Of course, my angel, of course.

PAPAGENO *(taking a drink)*

Ugh, water! Here, old girl, come and sit by me. Tell me, how old are you?

CRONE

Eighteen years and two minutes.

PAPAGENO

Eighty years and two minutes.

CRONE

Eighteen years and two minutes.

PAPAGENO

Ahahahaha! Eighteen! Hahaha! Well, you are a young angel. Have you a sweetheart?

WEIB

Freilich, er ist zehn Jahre älter.

PAPAGENO

Um zehn Jahre älter —, das muß
eine feurige Liebe sein! Wie nennt er sich
denn, dein Geliebter?

WEIB

Papageno!

PAPAGENO

Ah! Papageno?! W . . . ? Ah . . . ,
Papageno? Ich wäre dein Geliebter?

WEIB

Ja, mein Engel.

PAPAGENO

Wie heißt denn du?

WEIB

Ich heiße . . .
(Donner)

PAPAGENO

Oi! oje . . .

The crone hobbles hurriedly away.

PAPAGENO

O weh! Nun sprech' ich kein
Wort mehr.

CRONE

Of course I have; he is ten years older.

PAPAGENO

Ten years older! That must be a passionate
affair! What's his name, then, your sweetheart?

CRONE

Papageno!

PAPAGENO

Oh, Papageno. What? Eh? Papageno? You
mean I am your sweetheart?

CRONE

Yes, my angel.

PAPAGENO

What's your name, then?

CRONE

My name is . . .
(Clap of thunder)

PAPAGENO

Oh dear!

PAPAGENO

Oh dear, now I shan't speak another word.

The Three Boys appear, hovering in the air. One has the flute, another the bells.

Seid uns zum zweiten Mal willkommen **The Three Boys give new instructions to Tamino and Papageno, but all Papageno can focus on is the good food that has suddenly appeared (track 14).**

SCENE SIXTEEN
Trio

DIE KNABEN

Seid uns zum zweiten Mal willkommen,
ihr Männer, in Sarastros Reich.
Er schickt, was man euch abgenommen,
die Flöte und die Glöckchen euch.

A table loaded with good things appears.

Wollt ihr die Speisen nicht verschmähen,
so esset, trinket froh davon.
Wenn wir zum dritten Mal uns sehen,
ist Freude eures Mutes Lohn.
Tamino, Mut! nah ist das Ziel!
Du, Papageno, schweige still!

The Boys vanish again.

PAPAGENO

Tamino, wollen wir nicht speisen?

Tamino plays his flute.

PAPAGENO

Er bläst! Blas nur fort auf deiner
Flöte —, ich will hier meine Brocken
blasen! Hm, der Sarastro führt eine gute
Küche! Nun muß ich versuchen, ob auch
der Keller so gut bestellt ist. Hm! das ist
Götterwein!

THE BOYS

A second time you are welcome.
You mortals, in Sarastro's realm.
He sends what was taken from you—
your flute and your chest of bells.

If you do not scorn this food,
then eat and drink of it with pleasure.
When we meet for the third time
joy will reward your courage.
Tamino, courage! Your goal is near!
You, Papageno, be quiet!

PAPAGENO

Tamino, shall we eat?

PAPAGENO

He plays! Go on, then; play your flute. I'm
going to apply my mouth to these good
things. Mm, Sarastro has a good cook.
Now I must see if his cellar is as good, too.
Mm; sheer nectar!

Pamina enters.

PAMINA

Du hier? Gütige Götter, Dank euch,
daß ihr mich diesen Weg geführt habt.
Ich hörte deine Flöte — und so lief ich
schnell dem Tone nach. Aber du bist
traurig? Sprichst nicht eine Silbe mit deiner
Pamina? Liebst du mich nicht mehr? O
Papageno, sag du mir, was ist mit meinem
Freund?

PAPAGENO *(winkt ab)*
Wir . . .

PAMINA

Wie, auch du? Liebster, einziger
Tamino ... Oh, das ist mehr als Kränkung,
mehr als Tod!

PAMINA

What are you doing here?
Dear gods, thank you for bringing me this
way. I heard your flute and ran towards the
sound as fast as I could. But you are sad.
Aren't you going to say anything to your
Pamina? Don't you love me anymore?
Papageno, tell me, what is the matter with
my friend?

PAPAGENO *(indicating to her to go away)*
We . . .

PAMINA

What, you as well? Dearest Tamino, my
only one ... Oh, this is worse than insults,
worse than death!

DISC NO. 2/TRACKS 15 & 16

Ach, ich fühl's **Here is one of those breathtaking moments in which Mozart's sublime gifts
defy words. Pamina breaks down, devastated by all she has seen and endured. She pleads
for Tamino to know, somehow, that her tears are for him (01:33). The aria's melody is achingly
beautiful, with delicate orchestral touches that heighten the impact of Pamina's grief.**

SCENE SEVENTEEN
Aria

PAMINA

Ach, ich fühl's, es ist entschwunden,
ewig hin der Liebe Glück, mein ganzes
Glück. Nimmer kommt ihr,
Wonnestunden, meinem Herzen mehr
zurück! Sieh, Tamino, diese Tränen

PAMINA

Ah, I feel that all is past,
finished is love's happiness!
Never will you come, hours of delight,
back again unto my heart!
See, Tamino, see these tears

fließen, Trauter, dir allein;
fühlst du nicht der Liebe Sehnen,
so wird Ruh' im Tode sein.

Exit sadly.

PAPAGENO

Siehst du, Tamino, ich kann auch
schweigen, wenn's sein muß.

Trombones.

Ah, das geht uns an!

Trombones.

Wir kommen schon!

Trombones.

Tamino, na eile nicht so, wir kommen
schon noch zeitig genug, um uns braten zu
lassen.

Papageno runs off behind Tamino.

The scene changes to the interior of the Temple.

Sarastro and the priests are assembled.

flow, beloved, for you alone;
if you do not feel love's longing,
my peace must be in death.

PAPAGENO

You see, Tamino, I can keep my mouth
shut, too, if I have to.

Ah, that's for us!

All right, we're coming!

Tamino, not so fast, we shall still arrive in
time to get roasted.

DISC NO. 2/TRACK 17

O Isis und Osiris! welche Wonne! **As Tamino is led into the hall of the pyramids, the priests sing this broad and moving chorus of thanksgiving to the gods for his deliverance. The key of D major and the burnished sound of the brass (with trombones adding to the effect) elevate the dignity of the moment.**

SCENE EIGHTEEN
Chorus

CHOR

O Isis und Osiris! welche Wonne!
Die düstre Nacht verscheucht der Glanz
der Sonne.
Bald fühlt der edle Jüngling neues Leben,
bald ist er unserm Dienste ganz ergeben.
Seine Geist ist kühn, sein Herz ist rein,
bald wird er unser würdig sein.

CHORUS

O Isis and Osiris, what bliss!
Dark night retreats from the rays of
the sun.
Soon the noble youth will feel a new life,
soon he will be wholly dedicated to our
order.
His spirit is bold, his heart is pure,
soon he will be worthy of us.

Tamino is led in.

DISC NO. 2/TRACKS 18 & 19

Tamino, dein Betragen war bisher männlich und gelassen The soothing voice of Sarastro helps
Tamino and Pamina bear their troubles in an elegant trio (track 19).

SARASTRO

Tamino, dein Betragen war bisher
männlich und gelassen; nun hast du noch
zwei gefährliche Wege zu wandern.
Mögen die Götter dich ferner geleiten!
Man bringe Pamina!

SARASTRO

Tamino, your behavior so far has been
manly and composed. You now have two
further dangerous paths to take. May the
gods continue to go with you! Bring in
Pamina!

Pamina is led in, veiled.

PAMINA

Wo bin ich? Saget mir, wo ist mein Tamino?

PAMINA

Where am I? Tell me, where is my Tamino?

SARASTRO

Er wartet auf dich, um dir das letzte
Lebewohl zu sagen.

SARASTRO

He is waiting for you, to bid you a last
farewell.

PAMINA
Das letzte Lebewohl!? Tamino!

PAMINA
A last farewell? Tamino!

SCENE NINETEEN
Trio

PAMINA
Soll ich dich, Teurer, nicht mehr sehn?

PAMINA
Shall I, dear one, never see you again?

SARASTRO
Ihr werdet froh euch widersehn!

SARASTRO
You will meet again in bliss!

PAMINA
Dein warten tödliche Gefahren!

PAMINA
Fatal dangers wait for you!

TAMINO
Die Götter mögen mich bewahren!

TAMINO
The gods will protect me!

SARASTRO
Die Götter mögen ihn bewahren!

SARASTRO
The gods will protect him!

PAMINA
Du wirst dem Tode nicht entgehen,
mir flüstert dieses Ahnung ein.

PAMINA
A foreboding whisper tells me that you will
not escape from death.

TAMINO UND SARASTRO
Der Götter Wille mag geschehen,
ihr Wink soll mir (ihm) Gesetze sein!

TAMINO AND SARASTRO
The gods' will be done,
their sign shall be my (his) law!

PAMINA
O liebtest du, wie ich dich liebe,
du würdest nicht so ruhig sein.

PAMINA
Oh, if you loved as I love you,
you would not go so calmly.

TAMINO UND SARASTRO
Glaub mir, ich fühle (er fühlet) gleiche

TAMINO AND SARASTRO
Believe me, I feel (he feels) the same

Triebe, werd' (wird) ewig dein Getreuer sein.

desire, I will be (he will be) forever true to you.

SARASTRO

Die Stunde schlägt, nun müßt ihr scheiden;
Tamino muß nun wieder fort!
Nun eile fort, dich ruft dein Wort!
Die Stunde schlägt, wir sehn uns wieder.

SARASTRO

The hour strikes when you must part;
Tamino must go on his way!
Hasten forward, your vow calls you!
The hour strikes, we will meet again.

PAMINA

Wie bitter sind der Trennung Leiden!
Tamino muß nun wirklich fort!
So mußt du fort? Tamino, lebe wohl!
Ach, goldne Ruhe, kehre wieder!
Lebe wohl!

PAMINA

How bitter are the sorrows of parting!
Tamino now must be on his way!
Must you go? Tamino, farewell!
Ah golden peace, come back again!
Farewell!

TAMINO

Wie bitter sind der Trennung Leiden!
Pamina, ich muß wirklich fort!
Nun muß ich fort! Pamina, lebe wohl
Ach, goldne Ruhe, kehre wieder!
Lebe wohl!

TAMINO

How bitter are the sorrows of parting!
Pamina, now I must be on my way!
Ah, golden peace,
come back again!
Farewell!

They all leave.

DISC NO. 2/TRACK 20

Tamino! Tamino! Willst du mich denn gänzlich verlassen? **Papageno, meanwhile, has attained none of the seriousness that has come to Tamino, and is still thinking only about a glass of wine and a pretty wife.**

PAPAGENO *(kommt hereingelaufen)*
Tamino! Tamino! Willst du mich denn gänzlich verlassen?

PAPAGENO *(comes rushing in)*
Tamino, Tamino! Are you going to abandon me altogether?

STIMME
Zurück! *(Donnerschlag)*

A VOICE
Get back! *(Clap of thunder)*

PAPAGENO

Barmherzige Götter! Wenn ich jetzt nur
wüßte, wo ich hereinkam! irrt umher.

He wanders about.

STIMME

Zurück!

PAPAGENO

Jetzt kann ich weder vorwärts noch
rückwärts, muß vielleicht am Ende gar hier
verhungern. — Schon recht! Warum bin
ich auch mitgereist?!

ERSTER PRIESTER

Mensch!

PAPAGENO

Hier!

ERSTER PRIESTER

Du hättest verdient, auf
immer in finsteren Klüften der Erde zu
wandern. Nie wirst du das himmlische
Vergnügen der Eingeweihten fühlen!

PAPAGENO

Je nun, es gibt noch mehr Leute
meinesgleichen! Mir wäre jetzt ein gutes
Glas Wein das himmlischste Vergnügen!

ERSTER PRIESTER

Man wird dich damit bedienen.

PAPAGENO

Merciful gods!
If only I knew where I came in!

THE VOICE

Back!

PAPAGENO

Now I can go neither forward nor backward.
Maybe I shall be here till I starve to
death. Well, it serves me right. I should
never have come on this journey.

FIRST PRIEST

Man!

PAPAGENO

Here!

FIRST PRIEST

You really deserve to wander forever in the
bowels of the earth. At all events, you will
never know the heavenly joy of the initiates.

PAPAGENO

Ah well, there are lots of other people in
the same boat! At the moment the biggest
joy would be a good glass of wine.

FIRST PRIEST

Your wish will be complied with.

A large glass of red wine rises out of the floor.

PAPAGENO	**PAPAGENO**
Juchhe! Da ist es schon!	Hooray, there it comes already!
(trinkt)	*(Drinks)*
Herrlich! Himmlisch! Göttlich. Ich bin jetzt so vergnügt, daß ich bis zur Sonne fliegen wollte, wenn ich Flügel hätte — mir, mir wird ganz wunderlich ums Herz! Ich möchte . . . ich wünschte . . . , ja, was denn?	Glorious, heavenly, divine! I'm now in such good spirits I would fly to the sun if I had wings. Oh, I've such a funny feeling in my heart, I'd like . . . I want . . . Well, what do I want?

DISC NO. 2/TRACK 21

Ein Mädchen oder Weibchen Papageno longs for his Papagena in yet another catchy tune, one Mozart borrowed from a long-forgotten song popular at the time. The glockenspiel once again makes a delightful appearance in the orchestra (00:38), creating the effect of Papageno's magic bells. At least once, Mozart playfully slipped backstage and surprised Schikaneder, who was onstage performing Papageno, by playing it during a performance.

SCENE TWENTY
Aria

PAPAGENO	**PAPAGENO**
Ein Mädchen oder Weibchen	A sweetheart or a little wife
wünscht Papageno sich!	is Papageno's wish!
O, so ein sanftes Täubchen	Oh, such a gentle dove
wär' Seligkeit für mich!	would be a blessing for me!
Dann schmeckte mir Trinken und Essen,	Then drinking and eating would
dann könnt' ich mit Fürsten mich messen,	please me, then I could be happy as a
des Lebens als Weiser mich freun,	prince, enjoying life as a wise man
und wie im Elysium sein!	as if in Elysium! A sweetheart, etc.
Ein Mädchen, usw.	Ah, can I not please even one
Ach, kann ich denn keiner von allen	of all the world's charming girls?

den reizenden Mädchen gefallen?	If one does not save me in my need,
Helf' eine mir nur aus der Not,	I'll surely grieve to death!
sonst gräm' ich mich wahrlich zu Tod!	A sweetheart, etc.
Ein Mädchen, usw. Wird keine mir Liebe	If none will give me love,
gewähren, so muß mich die Flamme	the flames will consume me;
verzehren, doch küßt' mich ein weiblicher	but if a woman's lips will kiss me,
Mund, so bin ich schon wieder gesund.	I will be happy once more.

The old crone comes in, dancing and supporting herself on her stick.

DISC NO. 2/TRACKS 22

Da bin ich schon, mein Engel! **The old crone comes back to flirt with Papageno some more, but we soon learn that things are not always what they appear to be in the world of *The Magic Flute*.**

WEIB	**CRONE**
Da bin ich schon, mein Engel!	Here I am, my angel!

Emanuel Schikaneder as Papageno in
a 1791 engraving by Ignaz Alberti.

PAPAGENO

Die Alte hat sich meiner erbarmt!

WEIB

Ja, mein Engel.

PAPAGENO

An dem Glockenspiel muß was hin sein!

WEIB

Mein Engel, wenn du mir versprichst,
mir ewig treu zu bleiben, dann sollst du
sehen, wie zärtlich dein Weibchen dich
lieben wird.

PAPAGENO

Ei, ei, du zärtliches Närrchen!

WEIB

Reich mir zum Pfand unseres Bundes deine
Hand.

PAPAGENO

Nur nicht so hastig, mein lieber
Engel! So ein Bündnis braucht seine
reifliche Überlegung!

WEIB

Papageno, ich rate dir, zaudere nicht,
deine Hand, oder du bist auf immer hier
eingekerkert.

PAPAGENO

Eingekerkert?

PAPAGENO

The old girl has taken pity on me!

CRONE

Yes, my angel.

PAPAGENO

There must be something wrong with the
glockenspiel!

CRONE

My angel, if you promise to be
faithful to me forever, you will see how
tenderly your little wife will
love you.

PAPAGENO

Oh, you tender little thing, you!

CRONE

Give me your hand as a pledge of our
union.

PAPAGENO

Not so fast, my sweet angel!
Such a union needs careful
consideration.

CRONE

Papageno, I advise you not to hesitate.
Give me your hand, or you'll be incarcerated here forever.

PAPAGENO

Incarcerated?

WEIB

Wasser und Brot wird deine tägliche Kost
sein, ohne Freund, ohne Freundin mußt
du leben und der Welt auf immer entsagen.

PAPAGENO

Wasser trinken? Bah! Der Welt
entsagen? Na, da will ich doch lieber eine
Alte nehmen, als gar keine! Hier hast du
meine Hand mit der Versicherung, daß ich
dir immer getreu bliebe, *(leise)*
solang ich keine Schönere finde.

CRONE

Bread and water will be all you'll get, and
you'll have to live without a friend of either
sex, and never see the outside world again.

PAPAGENO

Drink water? Ugh! Never see the world
again? Then I'd rather take an old hag
than no woman at all. Here is my hand
as a pledge that I'll always be faithful to
you *(aside)* until I find someone more
attractive.

The old woman is transformed into a young girl, who is dressed exactly the same as Papageno.

WEIB *(mit Papagenastimme)*
Das schwörst du?

PAPAGENO
Das schwör' ich! *(dreht sich um)*
Papagena!

CRONE *(with Papagena's voice)*
You swear it?

PAPAGENO
I swear it! *(Turns round)*
Papagena!

He is about to embrace her.

ERSTER PRIESTER
Fort mit dir, junges Weib!
Er ist deiner noch nicht würdig!

FIRST PRIEST
Away with you, young woman!
He is not worthy of you.

He drags Papagena away.

PAPAGENO
Herr mischen sie sich nicht in
meine Familienangelegenheiten!

PAPAGENO
You, sir, just you stop interfering in my
family affairs.

He runs after them.

The scene changes to a garden.

DISC NO. 2/TRACK 23 & 24

Bald prangt, den Morgen zu verkünden Another trio of chords brings us closer to the moment of truth for Tamino and Pamina. As Tamino is brought in to face the challenges of fire and water, the Two Armed Men sing the melody of the Lutheran chorale as a kind of chant (00:57)—an effect that sounds much like the music of Bach. When Tamino and Pamina are brought together, the atmosphere changes, and the purity of their love and the intensity of their commitment is palpable in the music (04:35). When the Two Armed Men join them, the four voices create a moving musical image of faith and hope. Then comes Mozart's most dazzling coup, a moment of truly amazing grace—the simple, mesmerizing march (08:25), flute and drums supported by soft brass chords, that accompanies the couple through their trials. Tamino and Pamina's successful completion of their trials is greeted with a shout of joy from the chorus (11:05).

The temple of the sun as designed by David Hockney for the Metropolitan Opera.

DIE KNABEN

Bald prangt, den Morgen zu verkünden,
die Sonn' auf goldner Bahn,
bald soll der Aberglaube schwinden,
bald siegt der weise Mann.
O holde Ruhe, steig hernieder,
kehr in der Menschen Herzen wieder,
dann ist die Erd' ein Himmelreich,
und Sterbliche den Göttern gleich.

ERSTER KNABE

Doch seht, Verzweiflung quält Paminen!

ZWITER UND DRITTER KNABE

Wo ist sie denn?

ERSTER KNABE

Sie ist von Sinnen —

DIE KNABEN

Sie quält verschmähter Liebe Leiden,
laßt uns der Armen Trost bereiten;
fürwahr, ihr Schicksal geht uns nah!
O wäre nur ihr Jüngling da!
Sie kommt, laßt uns bei Seite gehn,
damit wir, was sie mache, sehn.

Pamina rushes in, holding a dagger.

PAMINA

Du also bist mein Bräutigam?
Durch dich vollend' ich meinen Gram!

THE BOYS

The sun shines to announce morning,
rising on its golden course;
soon superstition will disappear,
soon the wise man will overcome.
O noble peace, descend to us,
fill the hearts of men once more;
then earth will be a heavenly kingdom
and mortals will be like the gods.

FIRST BOY

But look, doubt disturbs Pamina!

SECOND AND THIRD BOYS

Where is she now?

FIRST BOY

She is bereft of her senses—

THE BOYS

Sorrows of rejected love torment her.
Let us find comfort for the poor girl;
truly, her destiny is dear to us!
Oh, if only her young man were here!
She is coming, let us step aside
and see what she intends to do.

PAMINA

You, then, are to be my bridegroom?
Through you shall I end my grief!

DIE KNABEN *(für sich)*

Welch dunkle Worte sprach sie da?
Die Arme ist dem Wahnsinn nah.

PAMINA

Geduld, mein Trauter, ich bein dein,
baid werden wir vermählet sein!

DIE KNABEN

Wahnsinn tobt ihr im Gehirne.
Selbstmord steht auf ihre Stirne.

aloud

Holdes Mädchen, sieh uns an!

PAMINA

Sterben will ich, weil der Mann,
den ich nimmermehr kann hassen,
seine Traute kann verlassen!
Dies gab meine Mutter mir!

DIE KNABEN

Selbstmord strafet Gott an dir!

PAMINA

Lieber duch dies Eisen sterben,
als durch Liebesgram verderben;
Mutter! durch dich leide ich
und dein Fluch verfolget mich.

DIE KNABEN

Mädchen, willst du mit uns gehn?

PAMINA

Ha! des Jammers Maß ist voll!

THE BOYS *(to themselves)*

What dark words did she speak?
The poor girl is near madness.

PAMINA

Patience, beloved, I am yours,
soon we shall be married!

THE BOYS

Madness rages in her head,
suicide can be read in her face.

Dear maiden, look at us!

PAMINA

I mean to die, for the man
whom I could never never hate
was able to leave his dear one!
My mother gave me this!

THE BOYS

God will punish your suicide!

PAMINA

Better to die by this dagger
than be ruined by love's sorrow;
Mother! because of you I suffer,
and your curse pursues me.

THE BOYS

Maiden, will you go with us?

PAMINA

Ha! The measure of my pain is full!

falscher Jüngling, lebe wohl!
Sieh, Pamina stirbt durch dich!
Dieses Eisen töte mich!

False youth, farewell!
See, Pamina dies by you!
May this dagger kill me!

She is about to stab herself. The Three Boys wrest the dagger from her.

DIE KNABEN
Ha! Unglückliche, halt ein!
Sollte dies dein Jüngling sehen,
würde er vor Gram vergehen;
denn er liebet dich allein.

THE BOYS
Ha! Miserable girl, forbear!
If your young man should see this,
he would die for sorrow;
for he loves you alone.

PAMINA
Was? er fühlte Gegenliebe,
und verbarg mir seine Triebe,
wandte sein Gesicht von mir!
Warum sprach er nicht mit mir?

PAMINA
What? He returned my love,
yet hid his feelings from me,
and turned away his face?
Why did he not speak to me?

DIE KNABEN
Dieses müssen wir verschweigen,
doch wir wollen dir ihn zeigen,
und du wirst mit Staunen sehn,
daß er dir sein Herz geweiht,
und den Tod für dich nicht scheut.
Komm, wir wollen zu ihm gehn!

THE BOYS
Of this we must be silent,
but we will show him to you,
and you will see with wonder
that his heart is dedicated to you
and that for you he would not fear death.
Come, let us go to him!

PAMINA
Führt mich hin, ich möcht' ihn sehn!

PAMINA
Lead me on, I want to see him!

ALLE
Zwei Herzen, die von Liebe brennen,
kann Menschenohnmacht niemals trennen;
verloren ist der Feinde Müh',
die Götter selbst beschützen sie.
(Gehen ab.)

ALL
Two hearts that burn with love
can never be parted by human weakness;
in vain is the effort of their foes,
for the gods themselves protect them.
(Exeunt.)

The scene changes to reveal two mountains. The left-hand one is spouting water, the other is spitting fire. In each there is a grille through which fire and water are visible.

Two men in black armour stand in front of the mountains. Tamino stands at center left.

DIE ZWEI GEHARNISCHTEN
Der, welcher wandert diese Straße voll
Beschwerden, wird rein duch Feuer,
Wasser, Luft und Erden. Wenn er des
Todes Schrecken überwinden kann,
schwingt er sich aus der Erde himmelan;
erleuchtet wird er dann im Stande sein,
sich den Mysterien der Isis ganz zu weihn.

Tamino is led in by the Two Priests.

TAMINO
Mich schreckt kein Tod, als Mann zu handeln, den Weg der Tugend fortzuwandeln
schließt mir die Schreckenspforten auf!
ich wage froh den kühnen Lauf.

PAMINA *(von innen)*
Tamino, halt! ich muß dich sehn!

TAMINO
Was hör ich? Paminens Stimme?

DIE ZWEI GEHARNISCHTEN
Ja, ja, das ist Paminens Stimme.

TAMINO
Wohl mir, nun kann sie mit mir gehn,
nun trennet uns kein Schicksal mehr,
wenn auch der Tod beschieden wär'.

THE TWO MEN IN ARMOUR
He who wanders through these paths beset
with travail will be made pure by fire,
water, earth and air. If he can overcome his
fears of death he will soar away from earth
toward Heaven; and, once enlightened, he
will be able to dedicate himself wholly to
Isis' mysteries.

TAMINO
I fear no death, acting as a man
to pass through the way of virtue
unlock the gates of fear for me!
I gladly follow the bold way.

PAMINA *(from within)*
Tamino, stop! I must see you!

TAMINO
What do I hear? Pamina's voice?

THE TWO MEN IN ARMOUR
Yes, yes, that is Pamina's voice.

TAMINO
Happy am I, now can she go with me;
now no fate can part us again,
should even death be our lot.

DIE ZWEI GEHARNISCHTEN

Wohl dir, nun kann sie mit dir gehn, nun
trennet euch kein Schicksal mehr, wenn
auch der Tod beschieden war'.

TAMINO

Ist mir erlaubt, mit ihr zu sprechen?

DIE ZWEI GEHARNISCHTEN

Dir ist erlaubt, mit ihr zu sprechen.

The Two Priests go out.

TAMINO

Welch Glück, wenn wir uns wiedersehn,
froh Hand in Hand im Tempel gehn!
Ein Weib, das Nacht und Tod nich scheut,
ist würdig und wird eingeweiht.

DIE ZWEI GEHARNISCHTEN

Welch Glück, wenn wir euch wiedersehn,
usw.

The Two Priests return with Pamina.

PAMINA

Tamino mein! O welch ein Glück!

TAMINO

Pamina mein! O welch ein Glück!
Hier sind die Schreckenspforten,
die Not und Tod mir dräun.

PAMINA

Ich werde aller Orten

THE TWO MEN IN ARMOUR

Happy are you, now she can go with you;
now no fate can part you again,
should even death be your lot.

TAMINO

Is it permitted that I speak to her?

THE TWO MEN IN ARMOUR

It is permitted that you speak to her.

TAMINO

What joy it will be to meet again, happily,
hand in hand, to enter the temple! A
woman who does not fear darkness and
death is worthy and will be made an initiate.

THE TWO MEN IN ARMOUR

What joy it will be to meet again, etc.

PAMINA

My own Tamino! Oh, what happiness!

TAMINO

My own Pamina! Oh, what happiness!
Here are the gates of fear
threatening me with misery and death.

PAMINA

In every place I will

an deiner Seite sein.
Ich selbsten führe dich,
die Liebe leitet mich!
Sie mag den Weg mit Rosen streun,
weil Rosen stets bei Dornen sein.
Spiel du die Zauberflöte an;
sie schützt uns auf unsrer Bahn.
Es schnitt in einer Zauberstunde
mein Vater sie aus tiefstem Grunde
der tausendjähr'gen Eiche aus,
bei Blitz und Donner, Sturm und Braus.
Nun komm und spiel die Flöte an;
sie leite uns auf grauser Bahn.

be always at your side.
I myself will lead you,
for Love guides me!
It will strew the way with roses,
for roses are always found with thorns.
Play on your magic flute;
it will protect us on our path.
In a magic hour my father
cut it from the deepest roots
of a thousand-year-old oak tree
amid thunder and lightning, storm and
rain. Now, come and play the flute;
it will lead us on our terrible path.

PAMINA UND TAMINO

Wir wandeln durch des Tones Macht
froh durch des Todes düstre Nacht.

PAMINA AND TAMINO

We walk by power of the music,
cheerful through death's gloomy night.

DIE ZWEI GEHARNISCHTEN

Ihr wandelt, usw.

THE TWO MEN IN ARMOUR

You walk, etc.

Tamino and Pamina are seen on the right, walking through the fire. Tamino is playing his flute. As soon as they emerge on the left, they embrace and remain in the middle.

PAMINA UND TAMINO

Wir wandelten durch Feuergluten
bekämpften mutig die Gefahr.
Dein Ton sei Schutz in Wasserfluten,
so wie er es im Feuer war!

PAMINA AND TAMINO

We passed through glowing fire
and bravely overcame the danger.
May your music protect us in the waterfall,
just as it did through the fire!

Tamino plays. They are seen descending on the left, and after a while ascending again on the right. At once there appears the entrance to a brightly lit temple. A solemn silence.

PAMINA UND TAMINO

Ihr Götter, welch ein Augenblick!
Gewähret ist uns Isis' Glück!

PAMINA AND TAMINO

O gods, what a joyful moment!
Guaranteed to us is the joy of Isis!

CHOR *(von innen)*	**CHORUS** *(from within)*
Triumph! Triumph! du edles Paar!	Victory! Victory! noble pair!
besieget hast du die Gefahr!	you have overcome the danger!
Der Isis Weihe ist nun dein!	Isis' rites are now yours!
Kommt, kommt, treten in den Temple ein!	Come, come, enter into the temple!

The scene changes back to the garden.

DISC NO. 2/TRACK 25

Papagena! Papagena! **Papageno literally reaches the end of his rope in his comical longing for Papagena (02:40). His despair is interrupted by the Three Boys (03:35), who produce the woman of his dreams. Their encounter is enchanting; each is so thrilled to find the other that it is a struggle for them to even utter the other's name (05:13).**

PAPAGENO	**PAPAGENO**
Papagena! Papagena! Papagena!	Papagena! Papagena! Papagena!
Weibchen, Täubchen, mein Schöne!	Little wife, my dove, my beauty!
Vergebens! Ach, sie ist verloren;	Useless! Ah, she is lost;
ich bin zum Unglück schon geboren.	I was surely born to bad luck
Ich plauderte, und das war schlecht,	I chattered, and that was naughty,
und drum geschieht es mir schon recht!	so I got what I deserved.
Seit ich gekostet diesen Wein,	Since I tasted of that wine,
seit ich das schöne Weibchen sah,	since I saw that pretty girl,
so brennt's im Herzenskämmerlein,	I burn in my heart of hearts,
so zwickt es hier, so zwickt es da.	and love pinches me here and there.
Papagena, Herzensweibchen!	Papagena! Wife of my heart!
Papagena, liebes Täubchen!	Papagena, dearest dove!
's ist umsonst, es ist vergebens!	It is in vain, all is useless!
Müde bin ich meines Lebens.	I am weary of my life.
Sterben macht der Lieb' ein End.	Dying puts an end to love,
wenn's im Herzen noch so brennt.	when your heart burns so terribly.

He takes the rope in his hands.

Diesen Baum da will ich zieren,	I shall grace this tree by tying myself to it
mir an ihm den Hals zuschnüren,	by the throat,

weil das Leben mir mißfällt.
Gute Nacht, du falsche Welt!
Weil du böse an mir handelst,
mir kein schönes Kind zubandelst,
so ist's aus, so sterbe ich;
schöne Mädchen, denkt an mich!
Will sich eine um mich Armen,
eh' ich hänge, noch erbarmen,
wohl, so laß ich's diesmal sein.
Rufet nur ja, oder nein!
Keine hört mich; alles stille!
Also ist es euer Wille?
Papageno, frisch hinauf,
ende deinen Lebenslauf!
Nun, ich warte noch, es sei;
bis man zählet: eins, zwei, drei!
Eins! . . . Zwei! . . . Drei! . . .
Nun wohlan, es bleibt dabei;
weil mich nichts zurücke hält,
gute Nacht, du falsche Welt!

since my life has miscarried.
Good night, false world!
Because you treated me badly,
and never gave me a pretty mate,
all is over, so I die;
pretty maiden, think of me!
If someone will restrain me,
take pity on me before I hang,
I will let it go this time.
Speak up, yes or no!
No one hears me; all is still!
So then, that is your decision?
Papageno, step lively,
and end your weary life!
I'll give them another chance,
until I can count one, two, three!
One! . . . Two! . . . Three! . . .
Well, then, it is settled;
since no one holds me back,
good night, false world!

Papageno is about to hang himself when the Three Boys rush in and restrain him.

DIE KNABEN

Halt ein! o Papageno, und sei klug; man
lebt nur einmal, dies sei dir genug!

THE BOYS

Stop, Papageno, and be wise;
you live only once, let that be enough!

PAPAGENO

Ihr habt gut reden, habt gut scherzen;
doch brennt es euch wie mich im Herzen,
ihr würdet auch nach Mädchen gehn.

PAPAGENO

You may well say so and laugh;
but if your hearts burned hot as mine,
you too would seek a sweetheart.

DIE KNABEN

So lasse deine Glöckchen klingen,
dies wird dein Weibchen zu dir bringen!

THE BOYS

Then play upon your bells;
they will bring your little wife to you!

PAPAGENO

Ich Narr vergaß das Zauberdinge!

Erklinge, Glockenspiel, erklinge!

Ich muß mein liebes Mädchen sehn!

(spielend) Klinget, Glöckchen, klinget!

Schafft mein Mädchen her!

Bringt mein Weibchen her,

bringt sie her, mein Weibchen her!

The Three Boys bring in Papagena.

DIE KNABEN

Nun, Papageno, sieh dich um!

PAPAGENO

Pa-pa-gena!

PAPAGENA

Pa-pa-geno!

PAPAGENO

Bist du mir nun ganz gegeben?

PAPAGENA

Nun bin ich dir ganz gegeben!

PAPAGENO

Nun, so sei mein liebes Weibchen!

PAPAGENA

Nun, so sei mein Herzenstäubchen!

BEIDE

Welche Freude wird das sein,

wenn die Götter uns bedenken,

PAPAGENO

What a fool! I forgot the magic!

Resound, magic bells, resound!

I must see my dear sweetheart!

(playing) Ring, little bells, ring!

Send my sweetheart here!

Bring my little woman here,

bring her here, my little wife here!

THE BOYS

Hey, Papageno, look around!

PAPAGENO

Pa-pa-gena!

PAPAGENA

Pa-pa-geno!

PAPAGENO

Do you pledge yourself to me?

PAPAGENA

Yes, I pledge myself to you!

PAPAGENO

Then you are my little wife!

PAPAGENA

Then you are my heart's dove!

BOTH

What a joy it will be

if the gods are so gracious

unsrer Liebe Kinder schenken,	as to send us dear children,
so liebe, kleine Kinderlein!	such dear little children!

PAPAGENO

Erst einen kleinen Papageno . . .

PAPAGENO

First a little Papageno . . .

PAPAGENA

Dann eine kleine Papagena . . .

PAPAGENA

Then a little Papagena . . .

PAPAGENO

Denn wieder einen Papageno . . .

PAPAGENO

Then another Papageno . . .

PAPAGENA

Dann wieder eine Papagena . . .

PAPAGENA

Then another Papagena . . .

BEIDE

Es ist das höchste der Gefühle,
wenn viele, viele Papageno
der Eltern Segen werden sein!
(Gehen ab.)

BOTH

It is the highest joy of all,
to have many, many Papagenos
as a blessing to their parents!
(Exeunt.)

The scene changes to the Temple forecourt.

Monostatos enters with the Queen of the Night, accompanied by the Three Ladies carrying torches.

DISC NO. 2/TRACK 26

Finale **The Queen of the Night, the Three Ladies, and Monostatos try once more to defeat the brotherhood, but they are routed (01:25). Musically the sun begins to shimmer in a cloudless sky in the form of a noble hymn of thanks to Isis and Osiris (02:30), and the splendid E-flat major first heard in the overture now denotes the joy of the occasion and finally erupts in an allegro (03:41) that brings the drama to a heartening close.**

ALLE

Nur stille, stille, stille, stille,
bald dringen wir im Tempel ein.

ALL

Now softly, softly, softly, softly,
soon we will be within the temple.

MONOSTATOS

Doch Fürstin, halte Wort, erfülle,
dein Kind muß meine Gattin sein.

KÖNIGIN

Ich halte Wort, es ist mein Wille!
Mein Kind soll deine Gattin sein.

DIE DAMEN

Ihr Kind soll deine Gattin sein.

Thunder, and the sound of water.

MONOSTATOS

Doch still, ich höre schrecklich rauschen
wie Donnerton und Wasserfall!

DIE KÖNIGEN UND DIE DAMEN

Ja, fürchterlich ist dieses Rauschen,
wie fernen Donners Widerhall!

MONOSTATOS

Nun sind sie in des Tempels Hallen.

ALLE

Dort wollen wir sie überfallen,
die Frömmler tilgen von der Erd'
mit Feuersglut und mächt' gem Schwert!

MONOSTATOS UND DIE DAMEN

Dir, große Königin der Nacht,
sei unsrer Rache Opfer
gebracht!

Thunder and lightning.

MONOSTATOS

But Lady, keep your word, grant that your
child must be my wife.

QUEEN

I shall keep my word, it is my will!
My child shall be your wife.

THE LADIES

Her child shall be your wife.

MONOSTATOS

But hush, I hear a terrible rushing
like rolling thunder and waterfalls!

THE QUEEN AND THE LADIES

Yes, fearful is that rushing,
like the distant echo of thunder!

MONOSTATOS

Now they are in the temple.

ALL

There we will attack them,
blot out the bigots from the earth
with glowing fire and mighty sword!

MONOSTATOS AND THE LADIES

To you, great Queen of the Night,
shall be brought the offering of our
revenge!

ALLE

Zerschmettert ist unsere Macht,
wir alle gestürzet in ewige Nacht!

ALL

Shattered is all our power,
we are cast down into eternal night!

The scene changes. Thunder, lightning, wind. Then suddenly, radiant sunshine.

Sarastro is revealed, and Tamino and Pamina, in priestly robes. Beside them, the priests and the Three Boys.

SARASTRO

Die Strahlen der Sonne
vertrieben die Nacht,
zernichten der Heuchler
erschlichene Macht.

SARASTRO

The rays of the sun
drive away the night;
destroyed is the hypocrite's
surreptitious power.

CHOR

Heil sei euch Geweihten!
Ihr dranget durch Nacht.
Dank sei dir, Osiris.
Dank dir, Isis, gebracht!
Es siegte die Stärke,
und krönet zum Lohn
die Schönheit und Weisheit
mit ewiger Kron'!

CHORUS

Hail to the initiates!
You have penetrated the night.
Thanks to thee, Osiris,
thanks, Isis, be thine!
Strength has overcome,
and crowns as reward
Beauty and Wisdom
with its eternal diadem!

Finale of the 1967 production designed by Marc Chagall for the Metropolitan Opera.

PHOTO CREDITS

THE MAGIC FLUTE

Wolfgang Amadeus Mozart

COMPACT DISC ONE

ZWEITER AUFZUG/SECOND ACT

COMPACT DISC TWO